Journey Into Motherhood

D0434291

Journey Into Motherhood

Writing Your Way to Self-Discovery

Leslie Kirk Campbell

RIVERHEAD BOOKS
New York

Riverhead Books
Published by The Berkley Publishing Group
200 Madison Avenue
New York, NY 10016

Credits appear on p. 239.
Copyright © 1996 by Leslie Kirk Campbell
Book design by Laura Hammond Hough
Cover design copyright © 1996 by Walter Harper
Cover art copyright © 1979 by Imperial Wallcoverings

All rights reserved. This book, or parts thereof, may not be reproduced
in any form without permission.

Riverhead hardcover edition: April 1996
First Riverhead trade paperback edition: January 1997
Riverhead trade paperback ISBN: 1-57322-576-2

The Putnam Berkley World Wide Web site address is http://www.berkley.com/berkley

The Library of Congress has catalogued the Riverhead hardcover edition as follows:

Campbell, Leslie Kirk.
   Journey into motherhood : writing your way to self-discovery /
   Leslie Kirk Campbell.
       p.   cm.
   Includes bibliographical references.
   ISBN 1-57322-026-4 (alk. paper)
     1. Pregnancy—Popular works.   2. Pregnant women—Diaries.
   3. Pregnancy—Psychological aspects.   4. Diaries—Authorship.
   I. Title.
   RG535.C317   1996   95-25767   CIP
   618.2'4—dc20

Printed in the United States of America

10   9   8   7   6   5   4   3   2   1

Acknowledgments

In my own journey into motherhood and in my journey into writing this book, there have been many beginnings, each one marked by a special person who, by his or her very presence in my life, nudged me closer to the soul of my ambition.

I acknowledge and express great gratitude to Jaime, whose eyes reminded me of the tenderness and suffering that sit like twin cats at the bottom of our souls, opening the gates to a world so human I was able to bear children; to Archimedes, for making me feel so star-crossed young again; to Wilfredo, whose helter-skelter beauty awoke my fancy; to Lorena, who translated what my heart could not speak; and to Vittorio, whose revolutionary dancing on a moonlit tropical night gave me back my beloved Italy, connected me inadvertently and permanently with the politics of the Third World, and brought me a boy. Thank you, Michele Najlis, Tomás Borge, Giocando Belli, Sergio Ramírez, and all the other poets who risked a somersault in midair and landed on their feet. Thank you, Marta, for your sweet courage and your mother and brothers and sister and Cruz for being my family the summer I started my own. Thank you, Nicaragua.

I acknowledge and express great gratitude to my San Francisco family when Orlando was born: to Hilda Gutiérrez Baldoquín, gentle and devoted unraveler of racism and my closest ally during pregnancy and early motherhood; to Sally Amsden, who buttressed my whole being with the life of Frida Kahlo and launched her own progeny in concert with mine; to Michael Lynch, pipe-smoking father-for-a-day, who named my fetus Barney and wrote him his first poem; and to Graciela Pérez Trevisan, whose laughter brightens molecules into stardust and who enjoys her love of language as much as I do. Thanks to Yeshi Sherover Neumann, who taught me to share my soul with more than one heart and brought my son out with her hands into the light of day; and to all the women who surrounded me with blessings throughout my pregnancy.

I acknowledge and express great gratitude to my many teachers, whose teachings are the psychological and political backbone of this book: to my teachers and co-counselors in Re-Evaluation Counseling, who taught me how to listen, how to be an advocate for children, and not to settle for anything less than absolutely everything; to Bayard Hora Associates, whose workshops taught me to tell the flat truth, cross lines relentlessly, the power of choice, and how to let go so well that I continue to carry this wisdom and courage today in my body. Thanks to Carmen Vázquez, who told me my voice is important and must be heard with such soulful conviction that I actually believed it; and to all the women at the San Francisco Women's Building, who taught me that the personal is political and how to love myself as a woman. Thanks to Elizabeth Browning, who gave me guidance during the scariest cliffhangers of my journey into motherhood; to Jonathon D. Gray, who has blessed both my son and me with his absolute trust in each of us as well as in our family; and to the invisible women at TALKLine who have saved my life repeatedly.

I acknowledge and express great gratitude to the guardian angels of this book: to Gloria Thornton, who, without knowing me from Adam, unabashedly encouraged me to do my Journey into Motherhood workshops from the beginning; to all the pregnant women who explored the vast territory of motherhood with me and risked the knowledge that they deserve only the best: respect, love, and time to honor themselves by writing their way to self-discovery; especially to Lisa Moresco, my defiantly spiritual and committed sister in motherhood; and to Libby Colman, whose professional psychological study of pregnancy ultimately confirmed my own research based on poetry, patience, and intuition. Thanks to Felicia Eth, my unflappable and zealous agent whose idea this book is and who reiterated her belief in me year after year by never giving up; and to Amy Hertz, my patient sculptor/editor, who always inspired me in my labor by telling me she needed my book written so she could start a family of her own.

I acknowledge and express great gratitude to my longtime friends who often unwittingly charge me with strength daily: to John DeFries, who shakes mountains with the power of a single word, who envisioned this book with my name on it fifteen years ago and who, together with his family, planted the spirit of *aloha pumehana* squarely in my heart; to Erica Hunt, for aggressively cultivating her mind while mothering, her daughter Madeleine, her new son Julian, and for courageously paving the way; to Scott Davis, hilarious word-meister, for always remembering; to Nelson Foster, for teaching me how quiet love is; to Frank Cefalu, who jogged me into clarity, literally, for months; and to Vaneida White, whose sterling friendship and integrity ground me in good faith year after year. Thanks to Cathy Colman, whose thirty-five years of best-friendship made her the only one on earth who could have borne witness to my "lemon tree epiphany," which has opened the door to everything else; and to Thomas Schenkel, my earnest and enlightened companion, whose brilliant faith in me has magnified the moon into my room.

I acknowledge and express great gratitude to my blood family: to Bubba, who braids invisible threads of power into my hair; to my only aunt, Loreon Vigné, mother of cats, heroine of my originality, and endlessly generous giver of gifts; to my brother, Bruce, my lifelong creativity co-conspirator; and to my sister, Jamie, my dear teacher whose mind mines pattern out of chaos and reminds me, in moments of critical mass, to surrender. Thanks to my father, Burnham Orlando Campbell, who always said I could do anything and whose forty years of dynamic and passionate teaching remains, after his death, my silent partner in every class I teach. Thanks to my mother, Caryl Joy Finn, who has made me a survivor, granted me the great gift of gab, and whose boundless energy reminds me that the impossible is possible and keeps me young. And, finally, thanks to my son, Orlando, whose innocence and honesty are my constant teachers.

I could never have done it without all of you.

*This book is dedicated to **Orlando***
and to all the other children everywhere in the world
who will inherit our future

The one who has thought the deepest,
loves what is most alive.
—FRIEDRICH HÖLDERLIN,
"Socrates and Alcibiades"

Contents

Contents

Empowering Ourselves:

Being Ourselves:

Contents

❧ 11 ❧

Down Under:

❧ 12 ❧

Full Circle:

Journey Into Motherhood

Introduction

From the conception the increase.

From the increase the swelling.

From the swelling the thought.

From the thought the remembrance.

From the remembrance the desire.

—NEW ZEALAND MAORI,
from *Technicians of the Sacred*
edited by Jerome Rothenberg

Writing is an act of redemption. I wrote *Journey into Motherhood* to save my life.

When I got pregnant for the first time I was thirty-five and knew no babies. I never noticed them on the streets, in grocery stores, in overstuffed seats in the backs of cars, playing in parks. No one had ever formally introduced me to a baby. My sister had no babies. My brother had no babies. My mother and father had no babies left. No friends had babies. I have one aunt and she was breeding exotic cats. Not a baby on my block. No memory even of myself as a baby.

So there I was, thirty-five and single. I didn't even have babies on my mind.

Or so I thought. I went that summer to Nicaragua to teach English to workers in the Department of Natural Resources. Brokenhearted and celibate after a failed monogamous relationship with the love of my life, I had brought enough condoms for the entire army of this Central American country. Not for me, of course. Medical supplies. Condoms for the people.

That's when the miracle began. Suddenly I was noticing babies. And young children. Everywhere. I ogled them, photographed them, held them, danced with them. And then it happened. I got pregnant. By myself. In a foreign country. For the first time in my life. Standing in that dusty street, holding the white slip of paper with its blue stork that told me I was now two, I felt like Eve. No one had prepared me for this moment.

I was a writer, so I wrote. I wrote letters to my fetus. I wrote every day, *Letters to Matagalpa* (the town of conception). And an amazing thing happened. Against all odds and reams of rationality, I decided to keep this fetus. To feel it grow inside me, to watch it meet the light of day, and then to hold what I had grown in my bare hands. I chose to give birth and let another child walk the earth. Well, actually, *we* decided, because once I started writing, I was not alone.

Then the child my own writing had chosen was born. I had a son and I named him Orlando.

☙

From the conception the increase. From the increase the swelling. Slowly, every day, I fell deeper into the well of motherhood. Yet I knew nothing about it. Frightened, lonely, and sinking into negative images of mothers throughout history, I needed to give birth to myself as a new mother. Once again writing was an act of redemption. But no longer just for myself. This is when I knew I was pregnant with an idea, something to give away. I started journal-writing workshops for other pregnant women and new mothers. Together we trekked through the wilderness of who we had become and who we were becoming.

From the swelling the thought. From the thought the remembrance. That became the first trimester of the book's pregnancy. All those hours surrounded by women giving birth to themselves as new mothers through their writing while their proliferating bodies expanded ever farther into my living room. Until, one day, there would be a newborn in a plastic baby carrier breathing in the corner of the room. Then there was another. And another. And still we wrote. We had given birth to our children but not yet to ourselves. And that, I found out, was going to be the longest labor imaginable.

From the remembrance the desire. Becoming a mother is quite ordinary on the one hand. Everyone has one. On the other hand, it is an extraordinary journey, one of triumph and of struggle, of incomparable love and immense joy, a journey, I have discovered, as my son turns seven, with no clear destination, no visible end.

۞

Giving birth is a rite of passage. Being pregnant is a rich, fertile, and creative time. There is nothing more magical than creating new life in your own body and then watching it grow; nothing more special than rising in love with a new human being of your own making.

Yet pregnancy is also a time of transformation and deep questioning. Pregnancy is a deeply psychological experience. A pregnant woman's inner life is powerful, private, and often disturbing. After pregnancy, nothing is ever the same again.

A woman's journey into motherhood can be an exhilarating and satisfying personal adventure. Or it can be a time of denial, confusion, anxiety, and overwhelming feelings that never get sorted out. Over and over again, I have observed that a woman's self-exploration is critical to her overall health and well-being and that writing is one of the most effective and rewarding ways for her to achieve this result.

This book engages you in a process of integration and connection that will change your life. Integration of self is something most of us rarely stop to do and, as long as we are alone, we may be able to get away with it. However, when we are about to embark upon a committed long-term relationship with another human being as we do in choosing to have a child, self-integration becomes our responsibility. At that very moment when I know I am bearing the future, it is my responsibility to myself, to my child, to my world, and to my species, to clean up my act and to locate myself in connection to my personal and cultural history, my community, and the world that

I live in. I do this out of respect for all life. I know full well that I will reproduce the wounds I have not healed in every relationship. I know too that I can uncover where I am strong and pass this on to my child and the future of this planet. I know my power is that I have choice.

By using *Journey into Motherhood: Writing Your Way to Self-Discovery* to write your own journey, you choose to confront rather than to ignore, you choose understanding over denial, empowerment and celebration over succumbing to pattern and attachments, hope over despair. Nine months is not a fluke of nature. It is a strategy for survival. It is just enough time to prepare yourself psychologically, emotionally, and spiritually to responsibly have a child and become a mother. This entire childbearing year gives you a unique opportunity to achieve new levels of personal strength and clarity of purpose. This book gives you the focus and guidance to travel safely through the vast territory that is your magnificently complex inner life so that you can take full advantage of this opportunity for now and forever. Your words do not die. They will continue to bear witness to the miraculous process of creating life on earth.

This is your choice.

❧

Women's experiences of the childbearing year may vary widely but the key issues are the same: the common difficulty of accepting the reality of conception with its accompanying feelings of ambivalence and denial; the anxiety of entering uncharted territory; the disquieting feelings of being out of control of your body, your future, your very life; the intense fear of labor and childbirth; the "crisis" after birth—many women experience the "blues"; integrating your new mother identity with your old identity; and accepting your baby as a separate person.

Other common feelings and issues raised by women in my Journey into Motherhood workshops will be the same as yours:

- SELF-ESTEEM—How can I take care of a baby when I cannot even take care of myself? Am I good enough?

- RAW FEAR OF THE UNKNOWN—How much pain will there be? Will I die? Will my baby die? What will my life be like?
- FEAR OF REPEATING THE MISTAKES OF YOUR PARENTS AND THEIR PARENTS—How can I "write a story" that I've never heard before? How do I invent something really new?
- DEFINING YOUR OWN TURF—How will I deal with the expectations and judgments of others around me?
- RAGE AT YOUR OWN MOTHER—When I have experienced a negative model for mothering, how do I figure out how to do it differently, to redefine it?
- FEELING OVERWHELMED—How can I do it all? Be a good mother and achieve my personal goals?
- ISOLATION—How will having a child affect my relationship with my partner, my friends, with everyone I know?
- PREJUDICE—Mothering is not valued. How can I feel good about myself making this choice, especially if I choose to stay at home?
- CONFUSION—If mothering *is* valuable, why am I not prepared for it? There is no training. How do I ever know what's enough, what's right, how I'm doing?
- EXHAUSTION—How do I figure out how to get rest, how to get help when I'm too tired even to think?
- EMOTIONS—How will my feelings affect the child, in utero and out?
- THE FUTURE—How can I celebrate bringing a child into a world with such severe problems and with predictions of a low life expectancy for the planet ringing in my ears?

When a woman journeys into motherhood she undergoes a transformation of her identity and of her reality. This identity journey takes her through different phases. The focus of the first trimester, "Locating Ourselves," is to establish the premother identity of the self. In the second trimester, "Redefining Ourselves," she tries on the new identity "I am a mother" though it remains an abstraction, the caterpillar in the cocoon imagining what it will be like to be a butterfly. The focus of the third trimester, "Empowering Ourselves," is on the miraculous phase of actual transition, when the tadpole can both breathe underwater like a fish and swim with its frog legs like an amphibian, when the baby is crowning, half in and half out, when a pregnant woman feels the undefinable energy of becoming: "I am myself becoming mother." In the fourth trimester, "Being Ourselves," she experiences two stages in her identity evolution. First, with an actual baby suddenly on board, she feels her self (her old sense of self that she located during the first trimester) swallowed up by her undeniable identity as a mother: "I am a mother becoming myself." And finally, as she comes full circle in her childbearing year, she can say "I am myself and I am mother." Her identity journey is complete when she no longer experiences the old and new identities as a duality but rather as an integration. She is whole again.

This book challenges you to go to the root of what it means to be a mother—to explore, discover, and create your journey into motherhood for yourself. Each chapter engages you in a process of self-evaluation and self-definition through the written word. Working through these pages you face your fears, your relationship with your own mother, your nagging doubts about motherhood. You integrate your past with your present and connect with your own history. You explore the meaning of family and of having a future. You celebrate your life. And finally, in doing so, you create a foundation for your new identity, your new life as a mother, and for your parenting.

❦

Journey into Motherhood is organized to make it easy for you to use sequentially. The book is divided into four sections, each corresponding to the first, second, third, and fourth trimesters. Each section focuses on a phase of your journey into a new identity: "Locating Ourselves," "Redefining Ourselves," "Empowering Ourselves," and "Being Ourselves."

Each of these four sections is divided into three chapters. The chapters progress month by month from conception through the end of the fourth trimester guided by the chronology of the psycho-emotional, spiritual, and physical experiences of pregnancy. The chronological approach provides a convenient structure for your writing. **However, given the unpredictability** of one's inner life, you may well choose to go to chapters randomly, based on your own intuition and need, and do the writing exercises at your own pace. I recommend that you get an overview of the territory before embarking on your journey and that you then choose to explore topics as you see fit. Rest assured that there is no wrong or right way to use this book. Whether this is your first birth or your fifth, the issues raised in the following pages are the most important psycho-emotional, spiritual, and physical issues for you to confront at whatever stage of pregnancy or new motherhood you are in. Your journey into motherhood does not end with the fourth trimester and the end of this book. Coming to terms with your new identity as a mother is an ongoing process during which the themes suggested here will continue to be relevant.

In the first pages of each trimester section you will find your maps and travel guides: discussions that orient you to what is known by myself and others about the psychological experience of pregnancy and new motherhood, a wide variety of excerpts from the writings of mothers including numerous excerpts from my own letters to my fetus during my pregnancy, and the writing exercises themselves with clear instructions on how to proceed. In the last pages of each trimester section are your "Journal Pages," the core of the book. The Journal Pages are your brakes, inviting you to slow down your busy life for a while and listen to its heart beat. It is here that you will write your own journey, your own "book," capturing the beauty of this time for yourself and for your child and starting a journaling habit that will serve you well throughout years of parenting.

Every chapter includes writing sections connected to the theme under discussion. Many of these writing sections start with a "Getting Ready" exercise to prime the pump. Here you fine-tune your senses, aerobicize your imagination, access your subconscious, and generally warm up so you don't pull any muscles on your writing journey. Don't skip "Getting Ready." These exercises are strategically created and placed to guide you deeper into your journey and to revitalize your language so that your journal entries will be powerfully written as well as insightful. "Getting Ready" helps you relax and loosen up, invites you to get wild, even to skirt danger, while trusting yourself at the same time.

"Journeying" is what you do once you're warmed up, the heart of your writing journey. These writing exercises lead you through the labyrinth of your own emotions as they relate to each discussion, and guide you through a process of integration and transformation that brings you full circle on the anniversary of your conception. Your collected responses to these exercises will eventually tell the awe-inspiring tale of your motherhood journey, the whole truth and nothing but the truth, documented for your private consumption or, if you so choose, for all future generations.

Occasionally, throughout the book, you will come across a section called "Looking at the Map." I understand how chaotic and often overwhelming the journey on which your words are taking you can be, and so I have included these places, small rest stops for you to stop and look around to get your bearings. "Looking at the Map" helps you to locate yourself even as you are in process by reminding you of what you have just done and to what purpose and by explaining how your words have prepared you to go to the next destination on your journey.

At the end of every chapter is a section called "Letter to Your Child." These letters may seem difficult to do at first when your fetus feels more like a concept than something real. I encourage you to write them anyway. Not only are they a moving record of your developing relationship with your child, but they will actually catalyze and clarify that relationship, creating an unimaginable intimacy with the life you're carrying way before a real baby comes onto the scene. You start the habit of honest communication with your child and build an unshakable love that will affect not only your experience of your pregnancy, childbirth, and early parenting but also the experience of your fetus who will soon become your baby daughter or your baby son.

You may choose to use this book alone or to join together with other pregnant women in your neighborhood or larger community on a regular basis. No one understands better what a pregnant woman is feeling and going through than another pregnant woman. When you put more than two together, you create a vortex of expectant energy that is irreproducible anywhere on earth. The already unstoppable power of females coming together to write and tell their truths is exponentially increased when these same females are in the process of creating new life. The experience my workshop participants had writing alone at home and once a week together was, for many, the most precious part of their pregnancies.

All chapters in the book include writing exercises that would be appropriate for you to ask your partner, family, close friends, or any co-parent(s) of your child to do along with you. To do this journeying with other people who will be key players in the new baby's life can be an extraordinarily powerful experience for all concerned.

In the last few chapters you will find exercises that outline ceremonies to celebrate different landmarks of this rite of passage, the baby shower, the birth, or a naming ceremony. Ceremonies such as these, or any others that you create or that are a part of your religious practice, help you both to go deeper into your journey and to provide a conscious and caring community for yourself and for your child once he or she is born.

No matter where you are in your pregnancy, and even if you have already given birth, you can go back to the beginning. You are not only giving birth to a baby. You are giving birth to a new mother. And in this journey, you are not alone. We are with you. Myself, all the women who have contributed to this book, and the millions more who have taken pen to paper while creating the miracle of new life everywhere in the world and throughout history. We are with you.

Beginning a Journal

Journal and *journey* originate from the same Latin word, *diurnus*, meaning "daily." *Diurnata* means "a day's travels," or "a day's work," and eventually came to mean traveling from one place to another. *Journal* has come to mean keeping a daily record of experiences, ideas, and reflections for private use. You will be doing both: "traveling" by journaling daily and journaling because every day of pregnancy and new motherhood you are "traveling" to another place. Your inner life is on the move. How are you going to track it?

First things first. You have a busy life. When in the world are you going to write? Find a daily time that will be your writing time. Make it sacred. Make it a ritual. Unplug phones, burn a candle, sit on your porch under the stars, revel in the peacefulness of predawn. One half hour every day. Longer if you can (the longer you can manage to spend in one sitting, the deeper you can go). Whatever it is, commit to it. Your quiet time of writing and self-integration will be the most important minutes you spend as you journey into motherhood. Remind yourself often that every human being must learn to stop and pay attention in order to see.

Still, neither a pregnant working woman nor a mother with a new baby has the luxury of writing for hours. Relax. The writing exercises are set up so that if you were to explore two to three questions each week, you could easily complete them within a year. You may well begin your journal in your second month of pregnancy, when you confirm that you are pregnant, or later, when you have made a clear choice to keep your child. At whatever point you begin, pace yourself. When you write in your journal, write as if you were dying. Feel the urgency and the significance of the work you are doing. Hold nothing back. Remember that while you are giving birth to your child, you are rebirthing you. Your old identity really *is* changing. Nothing will ever be quite the same.

Second question: What do you write? This book guides you through the expected dilemmas of pregnancy throughout the childbearing year. What you write will be the answers to the questions you need to ask.

Third question—and this may be the scariest question of all: How do you write? You may question your ability to write at all. Luckily for you, journaling is failsafe. "Getting Ready" will warm you up, get your writing muscles into gear, and then off you'll go, fancy free, your pen dancing across these pages. There is no such thing as not writing well in a journal. You are after truth, not publication. When you are getting at the heart of what needs to be said, your handwriting doesn't need to be beautiful either. Cross-outs are welcome. Tears and tea stains, too.

Writing is the most honest form of communication. It needn't be framed for anyone, not your husband, your therapist, your grocer, or your priest. You are writing for you and you only. Remember that whatever you write is what you need to write. Don't judge or censor it. Trust first thoughts. Not unlike alchemy, the exact words you choose to put down in that exact order will make the biggest difference. What is finally most precious comes from what is most simple. Call it the writing faith.

Do you remember that automated carnival game where you put in a quarter and awkwardly, from the outside of the big glass box, guide a crane over a pile of small toys? And no matter how much you long to pick up that cute yellow plastic watch, you get the gooey lime-green spider one more time? Or come up completely empty-handed? Discovering yourself through writing is very much like that game. You do better when you close your eyes and trust. Relax. Let go of wanting anything too much. Instead, let your intuition quietly land on the image it desires without directing it. Let it pick up that single image (whether your conscious mind wants that image or not) out of your endless pile of possible images. Pick up your pen and write it down. Then close your eyes and do it again. Pretty soon you will have a list of potent, vital, resonating images that speak to you, teach you, and move you mysteriously with their beauty. Later, you will look back and say, "Wow! Did I write that?" Then you will be silent for a moment as the meaning of your own words penetrates you. You will nod your head mightily, amused and amazed at your own brilliance, and say quietly to yourself, "Yes, that is exactly how I felt."

Annie Dillard answers the question "Who will teach me to write?" in *The Writing Life* like this:

> The page, the page, that eternal blankness, the blankness of eternity which you cover slowly, affirming time's scrawl as a right and your daring as necessity; the page, which you cover woodenly, ruining it, but asserting your freedom and power to act, acknowledging that you ruin everything you touch but touching it nevertheless, because acting is better than being here in mere opacity; the page, which you cover slowly with the crabbed thread of your gut; the page in the purity of its possibilities; the page of your death, against which you pit such flawed excellences as you can muster with all your life's strength: that page will teach you to write.

Journal writing is not just for writers. Anyone can write. Writing is always truest when it comes from the beginner's mind: fresh, surprising, engaged, and unself-conscious. As novelist Isabelle Allende said at a writing conference, "Writing is not such a great deal; it's just sitting there and doing. It's very joyful and simple."

As you begin your journal, you will discover the power of the written word. Writing clears the mind. It challenges you to be completely honest and to risk going as deep as humanly possible to discover the truth. It guides your energy inward and permits you to be meditative in the midst of a hectic, busy life. Out of this focus come clarity, vision, goals, actions to take.

Writing allows you to be totally free to express your emotions and to understand them by giving you a voice to convey your experiences during this miraculous time of human creation. Well suited to locating humor in the nooks and crannies where you least expect it, writing involuntarily grants you a multifaceted perspective on your situation and, as a fringe benefit, results in something special to leave for your child. In both the short and long run, writing is consistently therapeutic (and a lot cheaper than therapy!). Your written journey into motherhood releases energy that has been stuck in negative or unhealthy thinking or behaviors and, in fact, generates energy so that you have more than you had before.

Bon voyage!

Locating Ourselves

Your First Trimester

Weeks 1–13

"I am myself."

Human beings need to feel rooted in their own identity before they can contemplate transforming into something new. This is the purpose of the first trimester. Unlike the second and third trimesters, the first three months of pregnancy are a private and internal time. Nothing shows and so everything can be secret. Conception, baby, becoming a mother—none of it seems quite real. You even look like yourself, the self you were before the fraction of a second when your egg met its match. Yet in those private places where no one can see, everything has changed. The hormones resonate like music, both harmonious and discordant, in your emotional sphere; the psyche is morphing in spite of itself; and divine spirit suddenly runs like a river beside you.

In the following three chapters, "Diving In and Positioning Ourselves," "Our Intelligent Bodies," and "Back to Our Roots," you will take advantage of this private time to locate yourself in time and space spiritually, psychologically, physically, and historically, defining yourself in the context of your premother identity. You will listen to your intelligent body and gather your emotions like rain into buckets. Your own words will locate you on your life map, marking it off and claiming it. You will establish your point of departure. Who have you been up until now? Where have you come from? And who are you now as you stand at this crossroad?

You are yourself. . . .

One

Diving In and Positioning Ourselves

Your First Month

A garden looks no different

after seeds are planted

not for a while.

I feel no different

you are yet tiny

but you will grow like cornstalks

heavy for my soil

I am not ready

this winter is long

cold

without spring greening

and rush of river water

my soil cannot sustain you

I shall need the summer

time

to drink my sun

to let the river flow within

to fill my breasts with berries, fresh-picked

I will be rich and full

and give you everything.

I will believe in you

by summer.

——MARY ELLIS PETERSON,
"Conception"

"I'll believe it when I see it" is our usual comment in the face of anything extraordinary. The same goes for your little one, so tiny as she floats in her amniotic fluid that you cannot see or feel her and can't quite believe that she is really there. Know thyself and thou shalt know thy child. The first miles of your journey locate you emotionally in regard to how you feel about your pregnancy, position you in time psychologically and spiritually, and begin to unravel your dreams. By the end of this chapter, you will have a deeper awareness of who you are in every dimension. With the shards of your experience coalesced into a single identity, you will be able to speak to that tiny other you can hardly believe in.

1. On the Road:
Beginning Our Journey

It is now, when the whole jar

of humidity has been poured on me

like wet petals, and there is no question

of dryness anywhere, that I am most close

to everything alive: the wet breath

that links leaves and sky to my lungs

reaches deep inside my body and stirs

the silent seeds of all I hold dear,

and you, like the powerful muscle

we call heart, grow stronger within me.

——JOAN ROHR MYERS,
"Fertility"

There is a beginning to everything, real or invented. The beginning of your journey into motherhood began either when you conceived of having this child or when you conceived the child itself. If your pregnancy was planned, there was a point when you and your partner conceived of the idea of having a child, whether a first child, or a sibling. There may have been day-dreams, night dreams, conversations, undeniable symbols that you noticed in your path, a strong suggestion from a respected person, a family member, community member, or friend. Maybe you always knew that you would have a child one day and you can remember back to where that road began—a photograph, an incident, a secret revelation in elementary school, in high school, in the middle of the night. Knowledge of this kind often comes to us in odd ways and when we least expect it. Regardless of where and when your journey into motherhood began, there has been a road leading you to this moment. It may have woven in and out of other roads you traveled, fading at times, even disappearing completely for long stretches, but it was there to help you find your footing when the time came. And now the time has come.

Or perhaps, like mine, your conception was not planned at all. Life is complicated with its unexpected twists and turns.

Planned or unplanned, this is where your story begins, with creation. Right now, quietly, invisibly within you, you are creating. It is time for you to begin the creation of your book, to begin to express the complexity of your own experience in your own words, in your own way. This is the book that you are writing for yourself and for your child so that you can give a healthy birth to both.

THE BEGINNING OF ALL LIFE. In this section, you will have a chance to imagine the majesty of creation on a universal scale in your own genesis story. Imagining the origin of all things places you at the heart of the miracle of conception. You are not simply a reproducer of your species. You are part of something far more ancient. The astounding circumstances that allow all life to begin—a first electron, a first atom, be it God or some other miracle—boggles the mind. To allow yourself to feel that moment in your own imagination puts you in touch with the mystery of life itself and prepares you for the spiritual aspects of your journey into motherhood.

THE BEGINNING OF YOUR JOURNEY INTO MOTHERHOOD. You will wend your way back in your own life to where the first seeds of giving birth were planted. Origins guide us. Discovering the mysterious ways in which each woman awakens to motherhood gives us a deeper and more complete understanding of the path we are on, and provides us with a sense of purpose, even destiny. Think about every journey you've ever been on. It never started like a one-hundred-yard dash, your feet firmly planted in metal blocks waiting for the gun to go off. There is a preamble to every story. And a preamble to every preamble, providing us with context and direction.

In *The Life Within*, Jean Hegland wrote: "It is a grand mixture of precision and fluke, an intricate series of chances that mark our beginnings." You will write the story of the conception of your child—that magical moment when human life begins as one single cell. The circumstances of that conception, of those landmark moments, will affect the way you experience your entire pregnancy. If the details felt positive and healthy, remembering them will connect you with the joy and romance with which this journey begins. If, instead, the circumstances of the conception felt negative or confusing, remembering them with your words will help to heal the hurt and put the event in perspective so that these moments don't become a shadow darkening your pregnancy.

Going back to the beginning helps us to locate ourselves in time and space, and to recognize our participation in the grand scale of all creation. Going back to the beginning allows us to integrate conception, that inexplicable intersection of pure spirit and pure carnality, of biology and chance into the mythic reality of our own lives.

Remember, as you begin your writing journey through motherhood, that there is no right or wrong in what you write or how you write it. This journal is your private place, a place where you can write anything and everything. Trust that what you write is what you need to write. Trust yourself as you traverse the territory. Trust your words.

Dedicating Your Journal

A dedication refers to something you set aside for a specific purpose or use. A dedication is a proclamation of devotion and of commitment to that purpose. Write a dedication for your motherhood journal. What do you want to discover, accomplish, or fullfill by way of this written journal? In honor of yourself, take time now to proclaim your purpose in your own words.

> I am a mother, and a mother-to-be, and a wife, and most important yet most often ignored, I am me. I am Ann, a unique, thoughtful, creative individual and I don't want to be overwhelmed by my roles to the point of losing myself. . . . Through this journal I hope to reestablish my relationship with myself. I want to examine all the facets of motherhood and wifehood and just plain day-to-day living. It will be a way for me to stop, take a deep breath, and really think about what I'm striving for, what my life is all about. The days are so busy and full, we just barely survive them. It takes all our energy just to get through till bedtime. This journal will allow me to look at the meaning behind the struggle.

> —Journey into Motherhood workshop participant, pregnant with her second child, ANN QUENON PETERS

Getting Ready

We often look at myth to learn about beginnings. Select some music that, whenever you listen to it, is a door into another world. It might be classical, salsa, rap, rock, jazz, country, chants, or just a tape of the ocean. Turn on your music (or envelop yourself in silence if you prefer) and write your own creation story. Let your imagination run wild. Invent a story as if no one had ever told you anything about creation. It may be sacred or profane, solemn or humorous. Where did the stars come from, the sun, the moon, the planets? Where did people come from, animals, plants, oceans, mountains? Look at the big picture. How did it all begin? Don't think. Just write freely until the cosmos distills its shape, or shapelessness, in front of you.

> It was a giant named First Woman who created humankind. Long ago, when the world was young, she spread two blankets of mist upon the ground, and on each blanket she laid many things— white shells for bones, abalone shells for toes and fingernails, darkness for hair, sky waters for tears, lightning for tongues. Then, with the help of the winds and the Sun, she gave form and motion to those assembled bits of the world, and men and women arose from the mists.
>
> —NAVAJO, as retold by Jean Hegland, *The Life Within*

Journeying

1) Where did your own journey into motherhood begin? Allow yourself to go back to your first memories of wanting a child. Notice the moments, incidents, or situations when you felt a strong desire to be a mother. Or maybe the desire to have a child and the desire to be a mother felt like separate ideas until only recently. Go back through your life. Pay special attention to the time just prior to conceiving. Notice the symbols or signs that have led you

to this point. You can write it as a list: "When I was four . . . my cat had kittens in my bedroom closet," "When I was fifteen . . . I watched a cow give birth to a calf on a grassy knoll by the beach." "When I was twenty-five . . . in love for the first time, I noticed that little children existed in Italian piazzas." (Note: You may not see the beginning of your road right now. As you embark on this inner journey through writing, it will gradually dawn on you or, one day, while you're rocking your baby to sleep, it will come to you in a flash.)

> I am riding in the back of a pickup truck heading like a rocket through the fields to Leon and on to Ponelolla Beach. An eight year old Nicaraguan girl sits with me, sleeping in my lap, her head resting against my chest where I steady it against the rugged road and use my hands to protect her face against the cold wind. My heart melts. I feel she is mine. It comes like a large soft wave and rests there without going back to the ocean of its origin. For the first time in my life, I am a mother in my own heart. In this sudden unexpected world of mother and child, I feel completely safe. Something inside me changes forever. My bruised and battered heart opens up, reminding me how big it is, then closes again, or at least covers its face with its hands. But it is too late. I have already felt it. When she wakes, I photograph her sitting on the spare tire as we speed through the outskirts of Leon. I want a photo of my "daughter." Her profile is beautiful. Her long golden brown hair blows back as she faces the road we are all heading for. Later, after soaking in chemicals and slowly emerging out of nothing into an image on shiny paper, my child comes out blurry, a dream shot, as though the wind had light in it.
>
> —*Letters to Matagalpa*

2) Write the story of the conception of your child, the myth of its beginning. You may want to close your eyes and let your mind reel you back to that auspicious moment. Where were you? Was there music playing, a thunder-

storm, the aftermath of an argument? Remember the smells, the sounds, the textures. This is your child's creation story, the moment that put stars in his galaxy. If you don't know exactly when your conception was, imagine it. Where might it have been? Let your intuition hazard a guess. Make it up.

> Somewhere in the north Atlantic, just off the west coast of Ireland, the *Ambassador* cruise liner bucked and churned on every swell that rolled under its belly. My husband and I had decided eighteen months prior to the trip we were ready for a baby. By the time we set sail that day in Portsmouth it couldn't have been further from our minds. Encapsulated in my tiny cabin with the two separate berths as beds, I lay on one praying for relief from my seasickness. Finally my husband came back with a pill. We pulled our bedding down on the floor and clung to each other as the pill took me on a magic wool carpet ride to sanity as we slept. In the early dawn hours he pulled me to him as the drowsiness wore off. And so the sun rose on Bantry Bay, Ireland where the calm lapping waters caressed us as we caressed each other.
>
> —Journey into Motherhood workshop participant,
> KERRY SWANN FAIRRIE

3) Some women are infertile or are simply unable to conceive when they are ready to do so. If this has been your experience, your current pregnancy is a personal triumph the depth and complexity of which only you, and perhaps your partner, could possibly understand. Give yourself some time to give voice to all your many feelings about your difficult trek to this point, the hopes and disappointments, times when you felt like giving up, the ups and downs, thoughts of adoption, and the joy of consummation. In writing these feelings, you are clearing your heart and mind of past trials and preoccupations so that you can give unmitigated focus to your current bounty of *bon chance.*

2. Calling a Rose a Rose: Accepting the Reality of Conception

I am alone here . . . burgeoning with you. The fact of you inside me. The nascent reality of us. My apartment, which is small, feels huge and quiet. I lie like a tiny embryo against the wall in the corner of my room in the morning's dankness and grow, my thoughts multiplying like cells.

Maybe that bird wasn't a stork at all. It could have been a storm petrel or an ibis with a dead fish in its mouth.

—*Letters to Matagalpa*

For every woman there is a crossroad. One way leads to a child. The other does not. At every crossroad there is a choice to be made. You have made that choice. You are on the road to giving birth to a human being. Yet it doesn't feel real. The fact of it feels beyond your comprehension. Already you may feel tired, even nauseous, particularly in the morning. Still, you wonder, "How can it be that another life is beginning inside my body?"

If you find you are in denial, you are not alone. "No, I'm not pregnant," you may hear yourself say, "I just *prefer* eating dry crackers for breakfast right now . . . and for lunch and for dinner. . . . And anyway, my period is *always* late when I travel. No test is perfect."

Nor are you alone in your ambivalence, if that is what you feel. "The last thing I need in my life right now is a kid!" "There will be so much love when my baby comes . . . but I don't think I can handle all that extra work!" "Maybe this isn't the best time after all. . . ."

In this section, you will give yourself permission to acknowledge all the feelings you are experiencing. There are no right feelings and there are no wrong feelings. There are simply true feelings, the feelings that you actually feel when you look inside and notice them. Don't hide any. Diving in means taking the plunge, getting your hair wet. Here you can begin to define your issues about being pregnant: your fears, your doubts, your concerns as well as your happiness.

You define your turf by starting to really listen to your own voice.

Journeying

1) Describe the moment you found out you were pregnant. What was around you? Most likely, there were no double rainbows connecting your town with the next, no foreign landscapes to mythologize. Just the nutritional charts on the pale walls of your doctor's examination room or simply the bathroom mirror specked with old toothpaste. It doesn't matter where you were. It was a landmark moment. All the details are vivid inside you.

> I casually stop in front of a huge statue that stands in the plaza (I had never noticed it before). It is a woman carrying her small child in her arms carved in rain-drenched stone. Poised there, facing this statue, I feel like I'm flying. No one notices. Inside me a child! I refrain from any immediate judgment. I simply thrill in it. Like an astronaut in a space ship suddenly outside of her universe. Everything has changed.
>
> —*Letters to Matagalpa*

2) Dreams, fantasies, wishes. These things are abstractions. They live in the realm of possibility, a place you cannot touch. It is easy to say, "I want to have a child," as unfertilized eggs continue to drop out of your body. But what about the real thing? Say those same words after hearing you are pregnant. "I want to have a child." It is another story entirely. Ambivalence about actually giving birth to a baby is common. Expressing the ambivalence gives dignity to what is true for you without shame. You may feel ambivalent throughout your pregnancy and even after you give birth. Ambivalence may live with you as an undercurrent or simply come back to you occasionally like a high tide, holding you in its grip temporarily and then receding back into

the peacefulness of a single solution. Write the range of your feelings when you say, "I am going to have a baby." Include everything: your joy, your fear, your indifference. Tell it like it is. If you allow yourself to do this now and be honest, you will start a healthy practice of working through difficult feelings rather than holding them in. Whatever you are not willing to face stays in your body. And when you are pregnant, your fetus is part of your body. By expressing these feelings as they come up, we release our children from living out our issues. Understanding the spectrum of our feelings makes us mature, balanced mothers. Feelings of ambivalence after the birth will not surprise you. You will understand their origins. Write for thirty minutes.

3) Whether you experience emotional ambivalence or not and for whatever reason, every woman has issues about being pregnant, especially for the first time. Questions, fears, longings, concerns, you name it. Now is an excellent time to be specific about what you like and what you don't like about the fact of being pregnant and becoming a mom. This is your own reality check. Writing down the truth will help you to understand your range of feelings during this time and will give you a measure of clarity and wisdom to cope with them.

a) Write a list of everything you love about the idea of having a baby. What are the pros, the gifts, the benefits that you imagine will come to you as a consequence of having a baby?

b) Now write a list of everything you don't like about the idea of having a baby. What are the cons, the possible losses? It is particularly important to be honest here. No one ever said that giving birth is painless and that raising a child is easy.

4) You have some very exciting news! You're ripe with child! There may be those you can't wait to tell, those you're afraid to tell, those with whom you're not sure if and when to divulge this private information. First of all, there's the father of your child. Then there's your mother, your father, the rest of your family, your other children, your boss, colleagues, friends, grocer, etc. There is no question that they will all want to know and that, eventually, when you cannot hide it anymore by virtue of your immensity, they *will* know. Now, in the early weeks, your pregnancy will be invisible to everyone but yourself. Remember, it is your choice who to tell and when to tell them.

You are in charge. Is there anyone you are afraid to tell? Write down here why you are afraid or insecure with these particular people. This will help you to understand very quickly who you feel are your allies right now, who you can count on for support, and which relationships in your life need some work. These people will be your child's family, extended family, and community. Pregnancy will be a time when you can strengthen these relationships and begin to have better communication with these important people. Now is your time to coalesce a network of support for you and for your baby. Write down your feelings about telling each person, then write down how and when you want to tell them.

I need this secret I'm carrying, this mystery I can't understand, to resonate, to reverberate, to bounce back to me round and hard so that I can feel it in my hands like a basketball. I call my mother. I want to scream out the words. But first there is chitchat. So you're home. Yes, I am. So how was it? It was blah-blah-blah. Finally, I say I have some news. *And I say the words.* In English, in my own language to my own mother who bore me almost thirty-six years ago, I say it: I'm pregnant. I can't believe I'm using this word that I never, not once in my entire life, have had occasion to use, and here I am using it to my mother and I am referring to myself! I feel an unrepeatable onrush of innocent hopeful excitement. Expectant daughter to unsuspecting mother. What other simple communiqué from daughter to mother could possibly carry so classical a resonance? The first time can only happen once.

—*Letters to Matagalpa*

5) As you grow to accept that there is another person growing inside you who will one day be your daughter or your son, it is a good idea to name your unborn child. Poetry is naming the world, often in new and miraculous ways. Naming your fetus takes it out of the realm of gynecology and science and into the personal. Naming the invisible spirit inside you dignifies its ex-

istence, acknowledges its individuality, symbolizes something key about your relationship to it, and gives you someone to talk to. *Matagalpa, darling* is far more intimate and respectful than *embryo, fetus,* or simply *hey, you.* In addition, giving your fetus a name will help cut through any feelings of denial or disbelief that may linger.

Looking at the Map

You may not yet feel completely resolved about this journey you're on at this point. And yet, there is no doubt, you have embarked. You can see the ripples of water lapping around you, and the shore, though clearly visible, is beyond your reach. Water is an appropriate symbol for the emotions, fluctuating constantly, filled with invisible currents, immeasurable. You have been courageous. Calling a rose a rose has given you some clues into your rich and erratic emotional life and brought you closer to understanding how you feel about being on this journey in the first place. Once you have accepted the reality of your conception (even though you still don't quite understand what it all means), you are ready to look at the bigger picture. How does this landmark event fit into your whole life? You are about to bring a new character into the story. But what *is* your story? And who are you?

3. *Locating Ourselves: On the Map*

Whether you are seventeen or forty, married, single, on the brink of divorce, poor, financially stable, ready, or unprepared, you have been catapulted into another dimension. All past coordinates may seem irrelevant. You are in another orbit, unrecognizable, without clear direction, lost.

So who is this courageous woman embarking on a path into the unknown? What is her identity?

Before starting a journey, it is a good idea to make sure you have what you need, to know the content and weight of your suitcases, to look in the mirror, to check all your gear. What were the critical moments in your life, both sacred and profane, that have made you who you are today? This is what you carry with you, the contents of your complex identity, all of which will influence your experience of pregnancy, birth, and motherhood.

In this section, you will look through the contents of your suitcases to discover what, finally, is important to you. How are you situated in this special moment in time? What is your essence? These writings will give you a reference point for your changing identity, for the transformative experience of pregnancy, the biggest landmark in your life other than your own birth and death. When you get where you are going, that future you squint your eyes at but still can't quite see, you will want to look back to this to see where you were when you began.

Pregnancy is also a spiritual journey, difficult to locate, leaving no tracks. Someone is inside you and you are that person's bearer. These pages are your brakes inviting you to slow your busy life down for a moment and listen to its heartbeat. You are entitled to stop now and let yourself feel your role in the creation of life: one of the Milky Way's greatest mysteries.

Writing allows us to reflect on our lives. Out of this reflection comes meaning. Out of this meaning comes wisdom. Out of this wisdom comes our parenting.

Getting Ready

The way we locate ourselves in the world is with our senses. Our senses are our tracks to memory and to our existence in the present moment. Who are you right now? Imagine what your spirit would sound like if someone could hear it? For example: the roaring of salmon swimming upstream, a Ping-Pong ball on its last bounce, the center of a star. What would your "self" feel like if someone could touch it with her hands? Imagine if someone could taste your soul with their tongue, what would it taste like? What smell would it have? What nuances of color if you could hold it up to the light? What animal expresses the invisible qualities of who you are at this time? Start with: I am the sound of . . .

Journeying

1) Close your eyes. Look at your whole life as if from an airplane. Look at the roads, where they are smooth, where they are smoking with tar, where they diverge at intersections, and which way you turned. You have already experienced incidents in your life after which nothing was the same. These are the major landmarks sitting on the map of your life. They may have been victories or defeats. The birth of your little sister, the early death of your mother, your decision to be an artist at all costs, a spiritual revelation, a major car accident, a heartbreak. Write down five to ten specific landmarks and their aftermath—what happened and how did you change? Don't forget, your current pregnancy, the latest landmark in your life, is number ten on this list.

2) You have located yourself through the passage of time in the last exercise as you resurrected your past for yet another view. Now you will locate yourself in the present. What does the rest of your current situation look like?

Who are the people most important to you right now? (You got a head start into this process in the last section, exercise 4, when you wrote your feelings about who to tell and when to tell them about your pregnancy.)

How do you feel about your work, your career, any volunteer service you do, your hobbies?

What is your financial situation? Do you own your own home, or rent? Do you feel safe or insecure?

How do you feel about your health right now?

What is your relationship to your spiritual life?

Are there any other issues or concerns that define your present circumstance?

3) You have been locating yourself in your own personal history: rooting yourself in your personal past and present to facilitate the healthy growth of your personal future. Here you will locate yourself in "the times": the sociopolitical history and the state of the world in which you are giving birth. I was born in 1951, when the aftermath of World War II still reverberated throughout the world. My parents belonged, strictly as a consequence of historical circumstance, to a society that was still very much responding to that war, both psychologically and politically. There is no question that this determined my future to a large extent. The mind-set of all those who were survivors or even distant witnesses of the war, influenced not only my own life but the lives of a whole generation of boys and girls. History is Our Story. We make history happen and history has an impact on each one of us.

Bear witness to your own historical circumstance today. Have there been any major shifts in global politics? In the economy? What about in your country, your state, your community? What seem to be the most critical current events of this time? I spent my first month of pregnancy in Nicaragua surrounded by war, talking intimately with many mothers who had lost their eighteen-year-old sons and daughters to that war, experiencing the wounded and depressed psychology of a people embattled for years. This had a huge impact on my pregnancy and on my relationship to my fetus, and later, to my child. It is the fertile field out of which we grew. Every mother has her place in time and history. We are not isolated in our homes. We are connected to something much bigger and more complicated.

Describe the historical circumstance you find yourself in as you breed new life. Write for thirty minutes.

Looking at the Map

You have put yourself on the map of your life and on the map of the world. You have located your spirit just as you are in the process of believing in the spirit of life you carry inside you. Finding out who you are gives you a reference point through the turbulent identity change you will go through during your child-bearing year, helping you to find a foothold in the emotional chaos. You need this foundation before you can leap into the untamed territory of your psyche: the world of your dreams.

4. Our Dreams

Our dreams are extraordinary because they are boundless. Anything can happen there. Dreams allow our subconscious to work out our fears, doubts, anxieties, and confusions.

Pregnant women usually experience an active dream life. Our dreams are the theater where our powerful emotional journey into motherhood is acted out. In the first trimester, many women dream of harm coming to themselves. In the second trimester, pregnant women commonly dream of harm coming to their partner and have dreams about a stranger. In the third trimester, dreams are often concerned with injury to the baby—dreams about losing or misplacing the baby or being trapped in a small place.

Your dreams help locate you on your inner journey into motherhood. Remember your dreams now and throughout your pregnancy. Listen to them. Write them down. Your dreams are processing your changing identity night after night, just as your daydreams and fantasies are processing during the day. Your subconscious, your psyche, your imagination are all working overtime, preparing you on a profound level for giving birth and mothering.

Journeying

When you enter the world of your dreams, you are entering a world of association and symbol. Let your dreams help locate you on your inner journey into motherhood. Pay attention to them. Write them down. Allow them to inform you along the way. Dreams, like children, get excited when you pay attention to them. They come out from behind their couches. The more involved you are today with your dream life, the richer it will be tomorrow. To get started, write down any dreams you remember since your motherhood journey began.

I, together with hundreds of other people, come crashing down on top of city streets in a huge tall building that broke off at the floor beneath the one I was on. I remember the terrifying falling sensation. I remember pieces flying off the building as it fell and things shifting position in the office and the miracle of the coincidence that I was one floor away from not being affected by the incident. I remember the color of the building was light pink adobe with yellow in it. I remember no pain.

—the author's dream journal

One week later when I knew I was pregnant, I looked back at my dream journal. Reading it, I was astounded to see how much my subconscious knew while my conscious self had no clue. No dream can be taken literally yet the dream gave me an insight into the panic I was feeling, dramatized the physiological shifting that was going on inside my womb (the light pink adobe), and even possibly the subconscious terror I felt about a sudden traumatic shift in my identity, which could explain the passionate ambivalence I experienced in early pregnancy. At the same time, the miracle of the coincidence of conception (the floor below me didn't break off but my floor was "chosen") and the painlessness of the whole incident felt almost reassuring.

Dreams work full-time whether we pay attention to them or not. When we write them down, however, they inform us of a large percent of our human experience that would otherwise remain unknown to us, communicating through metaphor our deepest conflicts and emotions during pregnancy, and enriching our lives. Before you go to sleep, flatter your dreams into visibility by telling them you will remember them. As you move into your second, third, and fourth trimesters, continue to write your dreams here in your journal. There may well be an instruction there for you, an insight. Later, even years later, when you read them over, you will be struck with how brilliantly and creatively they have mirrored the complicated depths of this adventure.

Looking at the Map

Congratulations. You are well on the road. Just weeks into your journey you have located yourself in your premother identity, recording who you have been for posterity, for you will never be the same. You have established your psycho-emotional identity as a pregnant woman on the threshold of radical change before trekking too far into foreign territory. In doing so, you have strengthened yourself and your understanding of who you are and have prepared yourself to ride the roller coaster of a lifetime.

Positioned in your red vinyl seat with your safety belt on, you are ready to enter the physical world of your body.

Letter to Your Child

Close your eyes. Put your hands over your womb. Imagine your fetus. Now write a first letter to this human being growing inside you. Continue to write to him/her every month or more often if you like. Be honest with your child from the beginning. Whether you are expressing anger or eagerness, honor the bonding that has already begun.

> Dear Matagalpa,
>
> I wear a white dress. My skin is dark from two months of living near the equator. I am slender, perhaps I have even lost weight. There is no sign of you. I do not give you away. The light is bright, a bare bulb. And I am dancing. I am dancing into oblivion. I do not want to think about anything. Not birth, not death, not good-byes, nothing. The streets of Esteli are intensely silent but for the fragments of the music I dance to threading out over the roofs. Everything I now know, everything I have seen and heard—it is too much. You, Matagalpa, are too much. I try to dance you out of me, not literally, but out of my psyche already burdened with the souls my eyes have taken in and sick with the taste of blood. I am my dance. I am bursting

with the love I feel for the people I see around me as if through water. I am in love with life and drenched in sweat. I can not believe that I am in Nicaragua, one hundred miles from the equator, fifty miles from the war. I can not believe that you have come, a seed in my solar plexus, and that these rich souls, these lips, these eyes, these minds whom I have come to know, will disappear tonight.

—*Letters to Matagalpa*

Two

Our Intelligent Bodies

Your Second Month

I feel like an elephant lumbering among dainty women. I feel like a fishbowl with a huge fish lodged in it sideways. I feel like a rock that wants to be a peach tree, that wants to flower and bear fruit. . . .

—Journey into Motherhood workshop
participant, CHANDLER DOWNS

We hold everything in our bodies. Our memories, our fears, our babies. Our physical body is the visible manifestation of the psychological and spiritual maelstrom of pregnancy. Everything is changing. What more dramatic transformation of our physical form than pregnancy can there possibly be, other than growing into a baby from an embryo ourselves?

By now, your body is racing with hormones. Your physical symptoms, nausea, weakness, fatigue, can range from minor to disabling. Your body offers you your first taste of the unpredictability of pregnancy and its consequence, the raising of a child. Your emotions run close to the surface, threatening to overflow like hot lava. Your moods push back and forth like two teams of Vikings of near equal strength in a seemingly interminable tug of war. You respond with extreme sadness to small losses and with exuberant

joy to minor successes. Emotions, which you always felt you could rational-
ize before, feel so irrational now as to verge on madness.

Meanwhile, your sexuality is either frothing at the mouth like a rabid
dog or hibernating like a bear in the dead of winter. Nothing seems to come
in small doses.

Memories of birth and death rise up like statues, obstinate and unre-
lenting. Your identity is being shaken at its very foundation.

The entire territory feels unfamiliar. Yet no one has ever trained you to
be a cartographer of the unknown. How will you navigate?

You have your words.

1. Our Bodies

1

My breasts lay
on the whiteness of my table,
swollen melons
over ripe and out of season.

2

My heart
beat breaks the skin
of its own drum
desiring eternity.

3

Forty walking sticks
clacking like a forest of pencils
on the beach walk.
Two of them are my legs.

4

Like someone else's territory
my length of scar
separates me from what
I will never know.

—*Letters to Matagalpa*

Every day you look at yourself naked in the mirror and wonder who you are. Your breasts are swollen and tender. You may be vomiting, and are probably urinating more often. You may feel tired all the time. Your ankles may be swollen. Perhaps you are constipated. Your body feels as though it has been taken over. And it has. Not only are you not in the driver's seat now but you feel you will never again be given keys to the ignition of the vehicle that was once yours. Even if your body feels terrific and healthy, you are aware that it holds another growing inside it, small as a rosebud, eating your food, drinking your drinks, taking up heart space. You are in an intensely symbiotic relationship with someone you've never even met.

You may wonder, too, if your partner will find you sexually attractive as your body ripens for birth, changing your profile unrecognizably. Later, as your girth balloons, you will wonder how in the world even to have sex.

The road you're on is shorter than you think. Put on your jogging shoes. Pregnancy is an excellent time for you to learn to accept and love your body in all its forms, just as we accept the earth's body, fissures, cavernous mountains, volcanic slopes, canyons, swamps, and shifting sea banks

You can't afford to deny or reject your body. Your health and the health of your child are inextricably connected during pregnancy. You would be jeopardizing the health of your child as well as your own. Your body is intelligent. Listen to it. Negative feelings about your body can cause you to maltreat and neglect it. Developing a positive relationship with your body now will affect your state of mind throughout pregnancy and assist you during labor. Enjoy your girth. Remember the beauty of European Renaissance women, Chinese women of ancient dynasties, African and Mayan fertility idols, and Hawaiian queens—cultures and times in history when voluptuousness was desirable, beautiful, and sacred. Stay mindful that your body is preparing to perform the most challenging physical feat imaginable. Be good to it.

In the following exercises you will pay attention to your physical body. You will take an honest look at how you feel about it, how it's changing, how you take care of it. Your own words will teach you how your relationship with your body affects your health as well as the health of your child during pregnancy. Through these writings, you will face the good, the bad, and the ugly—your body image, your sexuality, feeling out of control.

You may well be surprised by the result. A pregnant woman who is unafraid to be completely present in her body, who tunes into the magical birthing process happening inside her and gives herself up to it, exudes beautiful, sexy, life-bearing power. She can't help it.

Journeying

1) Women's bodies have been revered, loved, photographed and painted, used and abused by cultures and traditions. How society has seen your body has affected the way you feel about it. Now is an opportune time for you to reclaim your own body. What was your relationship to your body before you got pregnant? A close friend? A lover? An acquaintance you wish you'd never

met? How much attention did you give her? What were your feelings toward your body? Did you skin brush and manicure her? Did you constantly injure her? Write openly in your journal about this relationship. Include what your body has taught you, both when you were paying attention to her and when you weren't.

2) Annie Dillard wrote, "A writer looking for subjects inquires not after what she loves most, but what she loves at all." What do you love about your body right now? Write down the body parts and what it is about that part that you love. Be specific. Include those parts of your body that may be adored solely by you. Maybe it is a birthmark on your elbow, the way your eyebrows meet in the middle of your forehead like a head-on collision, or the color of your nipples when you just come out of the bath. If you want, take a model's turn in the mirror before you start. See your body from a state of innocence rather than from the stereotypes of beauty given you by sexist tradition and media hype. Like a child. A child sees most clearly what is beautiful and special. Take my son, for example, who, when he was a precocious four-year-old described his imaginary angel to my sister in this way: "She's so soft," he whispered, "she looks like she's going to have a baby."

Write for fifteen minutes without stopping. Don't think. Thinking gets in the way of love and you are learning to love your body. When you believe you've run out of body parts that you love, keep going. Maybe there's a particular profile, the smell of your neck, the elastic surge of your belly.

3) If hormones were gold, you'd be a wealthy woman. Unfortunately they're not. Hormones are mavericks, so you may question your very sanity. Things you could count on before—your daily urination schedule and the power of your bladder under pressure, which foods your mouth desires and your body loves, when you need sleep, the size of your breasts . . . and your bras—are all unpredictable. Your sense of who you are changes daily because, in fact, your body really is changing daily, often dramatically. Write down every possible way your body has changed since your pregnancy started: externally, internally, body parts, body functions, sensations.

I gag when I open the refrigerator and have to turn away from [my husband] in bed. Nothing in the world smells wholesome, smells

right. Even the smell of my own hair disgusts me. Going to the grocery store is an act of courage. I sleep for hours, wake to retch on a
piece of toast, and then stumble back to bed, blank and heavy and
miserable.

—JEAN HEGLAND, *The Life Within*

4) Is there something about your body or your feelings toward it that
you feel could get in the way of birthing a child? Birthing is a process of
opening. A body that is hated or of which you are ashamed will not open
easily. Maybe you had a bad accident, or were molested, or feel your hips are
too thin. Later, when you get closer to the actual time of giving birth, you
will draw your body opening. Now, it is time to clear away any obstacles that
could obstruct the path of your child in delivery. Writing them down will
help you locate them and clear them away. Address your concern directly to
your fetus. Get in the habit now of telling your child the truth, your fears as
well as your joys.

My womb is tight, frightened. Then I see his cock. The man who
raped me. I see it clearly, detached from his body. It is outside of me
but it is inside of me. Matagalpa, I'm sorry. Eleven years ago he came
into your sweet exit dirtying it. It feels filthy to me right now lying
on my back in bed holding your round home in my hands. His cock
is still there, Matagalpa, like a rusty pipe with veins in it. There's rust
on the walls of my vaginal canal, bleeding flakes of metal shavings.
How can I dilate so much your head will come through, without exposing both of us to that terror and that shame? How can I open
myself like a mythical cave door sliding open at the sound of someone's magical words? Totally open. I have so often crossed my legs,
closing my vagina and all the doors behind it like shark's jaws, like
shark's teeth shutting on each other, locked tight.

I can wash your diapers over and over again, Mata. I can love it
and hate it. I can soak cloth, rinse cloth, dry cloth, rinse it again,

wring it to pulp, shake it in the wind, hang it in the sun. I can scrub it with a floor brush and boil it if I need to. But how can I clean your way for you?

—*Letters to Matagalpa*

5) If the way we take care of our earth has any reflection on how we take care of our pregnant bodies, both givers of life, then plant some seed, clean a beach, and write a pro-environment letter to your congressman. Good health is paramount to you and your baby. Write down how you are going to nourish your body. Include in your writing what you will eat, what exercise you will do (swimming is particularly satisfying to pregnant women), body work, yoga, anything you can think of that will cause your body to return your love. Also include what you won't do. Eliminate the things you do that are destructive to your body. It's simply a choice.

Getting Ready

SEXUALITY: Your changing body and your changing relationship with your body affects your sexuality during pregnancy for both you and your partner. Given that women tend to need more love and reassurance during pregnancy and that sex can be a powerful and intimate expression of that love, it is important not to ignore your libido and your partner's response to it. An unabashedly honest dialogue between yourself and your libido and between yourself and your partner about each of your sexual needs will help to avoid resentment and misunderstandings. You are not the only one you want to love your body.

Your journal is your equivalent to the high school locker room: uninhibited talk about sex. The best way literally to warm up to writing about your sexuality at this time is to write down your sexual fantasies. You feel shy? Remember this is your opportunity to let it all hang out. No one is listening except you. Pay attention to details. Smells, taste, sound, texture. Write nonstop. Refuse to be distracted. Spontaneous writing is like good sex. It gets better and better the looser you get. The pen disappears until there is nothing separating you from your lust!

Journeying

1) Humor is healthy, especially when the stakes are high. Write a funny personal story about sex during your pregnancy that illustrates how it has been for you. Something that really happened. Maybe your mother called at climax to remind you to be sure to buy fifteen receiving blankets instead of the required two. Or maybe it was a position you experimentally took to avoid crushing your new kid, which left you feeling as hollow as a Henry Moore sculpture and ended in disaster. Maybe it's simply a tale of insatiable lust, or the utter lack of it. Seek and thou shalt find. Don't forget to include all the juicy details.

2) You already wrote one of your wild, wacky sexual fantasies in the warm-up. You may have been alone in an African savannah, or with fourteen other people in a tropical hot tub, or with a fabulous face from the cinema screen. That's the whole point of fantasy. Anything, I mean *anything*, can happen. Now let's get back to the real thing. This one is for your partner (or, if you have none, imagine one). You are becoming hyperaware of your body, how she feels and what she wants. Write a scene in which your partner is making love to you. Say exactly where and how you want to be touched. (This may change throughout your pregnancy—be sure to let your partner know when it does.) Later, relax somewhere and reread it. Does it warm you up? Now leave it in a clever place where your partner will be sure to find it.

Looking at the Map

Your first trimester may well be when you feel most overwhelmed by physiological changes and symptoms. Particularly if you are pregnant for the first time, they feel novel, even shocking. And if you are one of the many women who experience morning sickness during your first trimester, you can testify that early pregnancy is no pleasure ride. Still, it is important to remember that physical change does not end with this chapter or at the end of your third month. Your body inevitably will continue to be a major theme for you throughout your pregnancy. Continue to write about it with the self-knowledge you have acquired by doing these exercises. Remember, the birth force is irrevocably inside you, yet you are its queen. As you strengthen your relationship with your body now, you prepare yourself for a pregnancy and birth in which you make the choices. You are *the* expert on your own ecology. This last section brought you back into your body, sacred keeper of your child. Now that you two are intimate once again, engaged, as you were at birth, in an honest relationship, you can ask your body its secret knowledge about birth. It knows what to do—after all, it was made for giving birth.

2. Birth

Life is full of miracles . . . that someone less awed by them can actually explain. The creation of human life in our bodies is one of these miracles. Biologists and geneticists can say exactly how the chromosomes of the sperm and the chromosomes of the egg attach in the uterus and grow per coded plan to become a baby human being. But for you, the pregnant woman, even if you are a biologist yourself, the visceral knowledge that there is a human fetus growing inside you feels absolutely amazing. That you, yourself, with all your worries, your wardrobe, your knowledge, theories and dreams, were ever four, eight, or even sixteen cells bewilders you. And that those tiny cells became a complete baby, which has grown into being *you*, with five fingers, two eyes, and all your organs working together to keep you alive and thinking until now and for decades to come, astonishes you daily. But that all this happens in your own belly, under your own skin, in an empty sac that you never even think about, is so completely miraculous that you feel like standing on mountain peaks and touching the stars with your magical hands.

During your pregnancy, you will feel, in your own individual way, in a moment of quiet solitude, when you are empty of ego and emotions, the spirit of the life conceived inside you. Conception connects you to all women who have ever conceived in every country on earth since the beginning of humankind. It connects you with the metaphysical, the spiritual, the nonscientific reality of life on this planet. This is your undeniable private truth that you feel only another pregnant woman can understand. Even if you are a very pragmatic and busy woman, the birth force will stun you, and, if you allow yourself to experience it fully, will derail you completely from your empirical tracks.

In this section you will explore and come to terms with birth in all the ways birth has affected you. You will remember your own birth into this world. You will come to terms with any previous conceptions you have had that did not result in birth, births that did not result in life, and babies given up for adoption. You will have a chance to express any concern you may feel about losing the child you carry now inside you to spontaneous abortion in the first trimester, when the danger of miscarriage is most real. You will begin to explore ways your own values will shape your childbirth experience.

Rebirthing You

Indiana August. Hot, humid, heavy. Indiana air has always suffocated her. She is twenty-one years old. This is her third pregnancy. . . . Sam hurries into the house and lifts us to her feet. Carefully and quickly, he sidles her into the flower delivery van. She remembers the heat of the morning and the thick scented geraniums and the white mum petals littering the floorboard. I am bashing my head against her bones. She covers her opening with white hands trying to prevent me from falling to the floor like a bald featherless sparrow falling from the nest.

—Journey into Motherhood workshop participant, DARLA RADCLIFFE

You are going to give birth in a matter of months. The concept feels novel. Particularly with all the information available now on what to do and how to do it, what not to do and how not to do it, you may feel as if this birth you are going to have is an experiment, that, before you, no one had ever given birth in the history of humankind. You may completely forget that your own mother successfully gave birth to you, and the mother of every other person on the street, in your office, on your television world news, gave birth to them. Let the words resound from the highest mountains and echo throughout the world, *you, too, were once born.*

Have you ever clearly and consciously imagined coming out slippery and hot from between your mother's thighs or being lifted out folded and bloody from a slit in her belly?

Birth is as important to face as death. Your own birth is key to who you are today just as the birth of your own child will influence his or her life dramatically. Your birthday is more than a date and an excuse to eat cake. It is a formative experience. What happened when you were born? Exploring your own birth through writing will bring you in touch with a myriad of memories and feelings. Even if, afterward, you feel unable to talk about it, you will understand yourself better. You will feel an indescribable compassion for your own mother as well as for your own baby as you give birth to her.

Remembering is reconstructing. You don't always know if what you remember really happened, or where it came from—is the memory a translation of a photograph? Was it pieced together from remnants of a story once told you? Did you make it up? Relax: when you are discovering "truth" through your writing, none of this matters. "It is emotional remembering," writes Toni Morrison, "what the nerves and the skin remember." You trust what comes to you.

Getting Ready

Find a photograph of yourself when you were just hours old or even a few weeks old. If you can't find a photo of yourself, cut a baby picture out of a magazine. Or observe a day-old baby of a friend. Take a good look at this baby so newly born into the world. This is a completely dependent human being, who, when he is awake, has his eyes wide open, constantly shifting focus. This baby is learning more in one hour than you learned in four years of middle school.

Close your eyes. Imagine you are that tiny baby. See where you are. Are you propped up on a couch, lying on your back on a cold, hard checkered linoleum floor, on your tummy in the prickly grass outside? Are you in someone's arms? Notice how open and receptive you are to everything around you. Your senses are heightened, tuned like violin strings. What do you smell, close to you or in the distance? What sounds do you hear? What textures do you feel under you, around you, with your hands? How does the air feel against your skin? What do you see? Can you see color? Can you see clearly or are things unfocused shadows of dark and light? How do you feel inside your body? Are there sounds inside your body as well as outside it? What taste do you have in your mouth? Notice the light. Notice what's happening around you. Is anybody there? What are they doing? How do you feel in the presence of the people who are around you? How do you respond? If you are lying in one spot, does someone pick you up? Who? How does that feel? Lying there, is your body moving? Stay wherever you are and keep noticing the smells, the sounds, the textures, shapes and colors around you. Notice what is moving, what is still. You are new. It is not the names of things that come to you but the qualities of things that you perceive: softness, vibrancy, sensations.

When you are ready, open your eyes and write spontaneously everything that you have experienced. Write in the present tense in the first person (from the "I" point of view), from your infant perspective. Stay with your body, your sensations, the qualities of things. You know only what you have physically experienced since you were conceived. You don't know that the man with the toupee is your grandfather or that this is the coldest winter in fifteen years. Write for twenty minutes. You may want to ask your partner or a friend to read the preceding visualization to you slowly while your eyes are closed, then leave you in solitude to write.

Journeying

1) Close your eyes and visualize your own birth. You may feel you have no clue, that you remember nothing. That is okay. Relax. Allow yourself to go back. Be patient with the mysteries of your own mind. Trust yourself. Your intelligent body knows more than you think. Write down whatever images, details, and feelings come up for you. One detail will open the door to more. Remember, you are reinventing your life. The accuracy of the facts is less important than trusting that *whatever you write down is what you most need to say*—in order to understand what needs to be understood, confront what needs to be confronted, and heal what needs to be healed. Write in the first person, from your own perspective. Don't analyze or edit as you write. Let it come to you. Be sure to include sensory memory: smells, sounds, textures, tastes, colors.

> I folded my arms into my chest and closed my eyes and aimed my head towards light, aimed towards voices. I heard a deep man's voice and he was telling me to come. Still no word from her, only a breathing that rasped like wind in a cold and lonely place. The man's voice was steady and gentle and sounded like a deep humming, and he spoke words, to me and to her, and I pushed myself toward that sound, away from the emptiness of that black-red cave that was so silent. The sudden cold at the top of my head, the surprise of touch, the strangeness of it, and then I opened my eyes and saw him, the man, he was so big and his eyes were a deep color, the same as his voice. He said hello, smiling at the edges of his eyes. I looked at him, talking to me, and I kicked my way out of her. She was still squeezing, still breathing like the wind, still saying nothing. Not even good-bye.
>
> —Journey into Motherhood workshop participant who had been given up for adoption, SUSAN ITO

2) Talk to the people who were present at and/or know about your birth. If your mother is alive, ask her to tell you everything she remembers.

Just listen without interrupting. Let her rediscover her own memories. You can learn as much or more from *the way* a tale is told as from what is actually said. When she has finished, ask her for more details. Often, with the passage of time, we only remember what we want to remember. Trust your intuition. Don't try to figure it all out. Ask questions that will require her to reveal even more. Listen well and take in all that she expresses to you by her words, her tone, and, if she is with you, from her gestures, facial expressions, and body language. Or ask her to write it down and send it to you.

Call or write to other people who were there. Get the story from different perspectives. Notice how you feel as they tell you.

How do these accounts compare with what you have already written? Write a second version of your birth based on everything you now know: your own intuitive account and the accounts of others.

I always hated the way they planned me, she

took the cardboards out of his shirts as if

pulling the backbone up out of his body and

made a chart of the month and put her

temperature on it, rising and falling, to

know the day to make me—I always

wanted to have been conceived in heat,

in haste, by mistake, in love, in sex,

not on cardboard, the little X on the

rising line that did not fall again.

But then you were pouring the wine red as the

gritty clay of this earth, or the blood,

grainy with tiny clots, that rides us

into this life, and you said you could tell I had

been a child who was wanted. I took the

wine into my mouth like my mother's blood, as I had

ridden down toward the light with my lips

pressed against the side of that valve in her body, she was

bearing down and then breathing in the mask and then

bearing down, pressing me out into the

world that was not enough for her without me in it,

not the moon, the stars, Orion

cartwheeling easily across the dark, not the

    earth, the sea, none of it was

    enough for her, without me.

—SHARON OLDS, "The Planned Child"

3) What have you learned about yourself as a result of doing these writing exercises? Are there ways you see that your birth has influenced your behavior, your personality, your identity today?

Write for as long as you need to about insights you have had in your own rebirthing work here. Notice if there were other key events that surrounded your birth also, slightly before or after. As you continue to go through pregnancy and do these exercises, more memories and insights will continue to come to you. Write them down. Notice how your life changes. Sometimes it won't be immediate but later, months or even years later, you will suddenly say, Ah-hah! suddenly recognizing a way you have changed.

I finally became cognizant of my belief that I would die young when I was pregnant at thirty-five. It was then, in a visualization I did of my birth and of surgery I had as a six-week-old infant, that it all started to fall into place. The doctors thought my mother was going to die at my own birth due to a blood disease she has combined with extensive internal bleeding that they recognized almost too late to reverse the consequences. I felt the panic, the danger, my own helplessness. At that same time, the doctors realized I had the same blood disease as my mother and that cerebral hemorrhaging could occur at any moment, particularly through thumb sucking, a habit which I initiated while loitering in my mother's womb.

After my son was born, I discovered that I felt in my bones that I would be killed when I left him at home, even for fifteen minutes, to go to the store with my car. That's when I started to do the visualization work and really pay attention to my carefully developed paranoia. After going back to that early experience, and other close calls I'd had with death, my sky opened up. I saw everything from a different perspective. Not that I was to die young, but rather that I had survived again and again. I was a survivor, a person who would live no matter what! I suddenly had a future. A future with my son and with myself. I realized that I would always come back to him. For the first time in my life, I made plans for the years to come!

—*Letters to Matagalpa*

Past Conceptions

"It's just going to be a bee sting," the doctor said
And it was,
a small tingle
quick pricking bubbles
under my navel

and then like a tiny

drinking straw

that went

in and out

with a barely audible pop

fast

so fast I almost didn't have time to whisper

"I love you"

and then

a Band-Aid unwrapped

with its plastic smell of childhood

and spread onto my belly

"All done," he said.

All done.

My child was inside

swallowing the fizzy drink

and it bubbled against his tiny tongue

like a bud

the deadly soda pop

(This little boy won't be sitting on the front steps

in his gym shorts

drinking Coke out of a green glass bottle)

while I lay on my side pinching the pillowcase

and wondered,

is he afraid?

can he feel my sorrow

flooding around him?

His father sat on a chair

next to the bed

and held my hand lightly

and I looked over his shoulder

into the dark slice of window

between the heavy curtains

and the child

jumped against my hand

leaping through

> *the darkness*
>
> *and then*
>
> *was gone.*

—Journey into Motherhood workshop participant recalling an
abortion required so that she could survive preeclampsia, SUSAN ITO

Losing a fetus or baby, whether or not you have actively chosen this outcome and for whatever reasons, can embed itself in your psyche as tragedy.
Unless a woman is communicating with her fetus, or carrying on a written
dialogue with him or her as you are in these pages, a woman may feel little
emotional attachment to the fetus at the time of an abortion or miscarriage
and may even make light of her loss. Yet a woman who does not grieve this
loss, who does not say good-bye to the miracle begun inside her, may not
heal or clear herself to give birth in the future.

Some of you have been pregnant before and have lost the fetus or the baby when it was born. I have had pregnant women in my workshops who have lost as many as four or five fetuses and have never actually given birth. I know of a woman who decided, after a few unsuccessful pregnancies, that she could only create a dead or bad or blighted thing. If you are holding on to losses or memories of a tragic birth in the past, the passage for a healthy, happy delivery may be blocked on both the psychic and physical levels. In honor of all life, clear away any repressed feelings of guilt, sorrow, or remorse that you are holding on to. Now is a time to speak to the "lives" that have been inside you—the "lives" that have never seen the light of day nor breathed the air as you do.

Journeying

1) Write a letter to any "lives" that you have conceived and lost, and say good-bye. Take your time. Start in silence recalling that time. Imagine the spirit or soul that was to be your child. If you cannot imagine it directly, visualize walking along a path and encountering a young child. This is the child who would have been yours if you had decided or been allowed to keep her. Express your unsaid feelings in a letter to this being. Start with *Dear . . .*

2) You have written to this "spirit" whose destiny was not to breathe on this physical plane this time around. Now listen to him. See if this being has anything to say to you. Close your eyes. Listen carefully without expectations or skepticism. Write the words down. Does this being have any gifts for you? What are they?

3) Given that miscarriage is not uncommon in the first trimester, write about any anxiety you feel about the possibility of losing the child you're pregnant with now. Talk to him directly. Tell her how you feel.

If you do have a spontaneous abortion, writing down all your feelings will help you to come to terms with this natural and tragic event. Say good-bye to this "spirit," too. Know in your heart that in every ending there is a new beginning that will reveal itself to you at whatever point you are ready to embrace it.

Childbirth

Childbirth is like a garden, a landscape you study and design—yet when the flowers you planted all come up, they never quite look how you expected them to look. What is important is to have a vision. What are your values, your priorities? How will you take advantage of what women now know about giving birth and how will you use this information to sketch out your own birth plan? How will your giving birth be different from your mother birthing you?

Early in pregnancy, when the reality of labor and childbirth still seem remote, is a good time to begin to explore the many different childbirth options and to clarify your fundamental vision of giving birth. What medical systems do you believe in? Where do you want to be: home, a birth center, a hospital delivery room, the beach? What environment do you want to create? What qualities, elements, and people do you want present? Who do you trust to make decisions for you if you cannot? Now, when the topic is not too hot, is the optimum time to start recognizing which factors are most important and to discover your own bottom line.

Out of your vision you will slowly create a plan. You will decide on a method of childbirth and start to build honest relationships with your doctors, nurses, and/or midwives. By starting now, you give yourself and your birth plan plenty of time to evolve into its final form.

Later on, you will need to negotiate this plan with your caregivers. You will need to communicate what you want to them confidently. It will be important for you to be clear with both professionals and your personal support system about your vision, your bottom line, and how you want to be treated. You are, after all, interacting with an entire medical system. Your plan will give you clarity as well as support. You are not a victim. You are a proactive participant in your own birthing process. Remember that you are the queen, the expert on your own ecology.

Still, no matter how much you plan your birth, and no matter how assertive you may be, the truth of the matter is that birth is a total adventure.

There are many extenuating circumstances over which you have no control, the main one being the life-force itself. Ultimately, your child will come to you in his own way at his own time.

Getting Ready

Given the unpredictability of pregnancy, birth, and childrearing, turning problems into gifts is a good habit to get into. Think of a time when a plan you had made fell through. For example, I planned to sleep romantically on the beach in Hawaii with my visiting boyfriend when I was twenty, but first the sand crabs invaded our sleeping bags, and then it rained as if there were no tomorrow. What did we do instead? We tried to fit ourselves into a Japanese compact car to catch some sleep, but after much futile shifting into a variety of configurations we suddenly burst out laughing so hard we couldn't stop. What did I learn from this? I learned that this man was a good choice because he had the patience of a saint and a good sense of humor to boot and that romance is in the eye of the beholder. Think of a time when a plan you had made fell through. What did you do instead? How did you turn this "problem" into a gift? Keep asking yourself this question and writing down the answers. Giving spontaneous answers to a question repeated several times is an effective method for self-discovery. The repetition ultimately cuts through the glib answer, the habitual response, the borrowed phrases, and leads to true revelation. Ask and answer the question at least ten times.

Journeying

1) Close your eyes. Visualize yourself giving birth. Regardless of what you know or don't know at this point about the options available to you, write down your ideal situation. Start with the values and qualities of being and interacting that are most important to you. Then visualize your labor.

Where do you want to be, doing what, with whom? Keep visualizing until you are dilated enough to go to the hospital or to prepare yourself for giving birth at home. Where are you now? What is around you? What sounds, smells, textures, colors? What are you wearing? What is in the room or the space? What position are you in? Who is there? What are they doing? Include things that you think might not be possible to plan, for instance, the birth time, the weather, the astrological configuration of the stars. Your vision is unlimited. Go for broke. Allow it all to come to you and include everything that you want. It may be very simple or it may be complicated. It doesn't matter. This is *your* vision. Write it down including all the details.

Now that you've got your vision written down, start to read up on your medical options. Talk to people. Interview midwives, doctors. Take your time. As you integrate what you are learning with the seminal vision you already have, start to write a preliminary birth plan. Become more and more specific. Include all the medical logistics, drugs and their timing, the kind of care you want. Answer all your questions in the plan. Include the what-ifs. What if your child is still not born two weeks after the due date? What if it is a breech baby? What if labor take thirty hours instead of fifteen? What would the plan be then? Allow your plan to continue to develop until you give birth. As you feel more confident about it, share it with your partner and others you want to be present at your birth. Fine-tune it. Communicate it clearly to your caregivers. You are using everything you know, intuit, and feel to design your garden. When all is said and done, it will exude a rare kind of beauty, a beauty you had never imagined was possible.

2) Take some time now to write about how you feel about your medical visits and about the way your relationship with your prenatal care provider—doctor, midwife, or nurse practitioner—is developing. Take responsibility for having the relationship be based on the values you wrote about in the last exercise. Continue to write about your prenatal visits throughout your pregnancy. Your writing will clarify what it is you may be missing and what it is you need to ask for. Always ask for what you need.

3. $\mathcal{I}$lluminating the $\mathcal{S}$hadows: $\mathcal{F}$ears of the $\mathcal{U}$nexpected

In this section, you will have the opportunity to address your secrets, your fears, and your superstitions. "At times of personal crisis, such as pregnancy," writes Libby Colman in *Pregnancy: The Psychological Experience*, "when the familiar patterns have to be changed, we are more vulnerable to fears of the unknown and of the irrational." Your emotions live close to the surface like hungry aquarium fish. By writing them down, you make them more understandable.

Don't begrudge yourself your emotional chaos. It is your spawning ground for radical change.

Getting Ready

Superstition and myth are people's way of feeling in control of the uncontrollable, of humanizing the unknown. Cultures around the world have invented much folklore about conception, pregnancy, and giving birth. What are the superstitions about the process of giving birth that you grew up with? I believed that a serendipitous sighting of a falling star late in pregnancy meant my labor would go fast and smooth. Which is what happened. What about your parents, your grandparents, your culture? What are your own? Some of your superstitions may also be your beliefs. It doesn't matter if someone else thinks you're absolutely loony.

> The Malaysians thought that if a pregnant woman shot an animal in
> the eye, her child would be born blind. . . . The list goes on, a multi-
> cultural catalogue of the ways a woman's experiences and actions, de-
> sires and fears can shape the flesh and spirit of her unborn: if she
> looks at the moon, her child will be a lunatic; if she craves strawber-
> ries, her baby will be born with the mark of her craving etched upon

its skin; if she curses, her baby will be born a freak; if she trips on a grave, her child will be clubfooted. . . . We have been told to avoid eclipses and madmen, spicy foods and wild animals, sex, heat, and too much sleep.

—Jean Hegland, *The Life Within*

Journeying

Physical symptoms such as nausea and fatigue are your first hint about how unpredictable childbearing can be, a clue to how much your life is going to change. Everyone is afraid of the unknown. Your journal is a place where you can tell the truth. You can write here what you might not be willing to say to anyone. Take the risk now of writing down your fears, big and small, in regard to your labor, giving birth, your relationship, your work, your life. Don't worry. Writing them down doesn't make them happen. It gives you permission to look at them and release them. They may not go away completely but they will not control or paralyze you.

Looking at the Map

You are doing an excellent job of weeding your garden. You weed so that the roots of the seed planted inside you will not get tangled in or strangled by unwanted growth. Some weeds, you have found, come out easily, their roots slipping up all in one piece from the soil as if they had never really wanted to be there in the first place. Others are more stubborn. If you don't use the right tool and dig them up from their roots, they come back again. Writing is your optimum weeding tool. Slowly but surely, your writing pulls the weeds up one by one, making room for the flower of your choice.

No one else can weed your garden for you. They would have to constantly turn to you and ask, "Is this a weed or a plant you want to keep?" Only you know the answer to that. Maybe something you feel you want to keep now will later be taken out. That's okay. You are the highest ranking gardener, green thumbs and all. Your vision of your garden evolves daily as you write.

Letter to Your Child

Write a letter to your two-month-old fetus, tiny as an apricot.

Dear Matagalpa,
I cannot feel you. I keep feeling for you with my hands. Sometimes I feel a pressure, or I imagine I do. Like the heather in Scotland—that incredible energy exuding from miles of rolling hillocks just days before they explode with purple heather in every direction. But now, in the mirror, no sign of color, not even a speck of lavender. Just the rolling green going on forever. Yet that desire to bloom, that anticipation of total transformation of the landscape scintillates the air.

—*Letters to Matagalpa*

Three
Back to Our Roots
Your Third Month

You know, they straightened out the Mississippi River in places, to make room for houses and livable acreage. Occasionally the river floods these places. "Floods" is the word they use, but in fact it is not flooding; it is remembering. Remembering where it used to be. All water has a perfect memory and is forever trying to get back to where it was.

—TONI MORRISON, *Inventing the Truth*

There is a first time for everything. A first kiss, a first child, the first word. And before that, the first human being, the beginning of life in the universe, the first mass in space, the first space. We are part of all that. As creators we are connected with all of creation. We belong here not only because we were born here but because we give voice to an unfolding of existence that goes back to the beginning.

The roots of our present and future reside in our past. Our children, like ourselves, are being born into a global village on a five-billion-year-old planet traveling sixty-six thousand miles per hour through space. We are born into and connected to concentric spirals of history circling outward into infinity: personal, family, community, cultural and racial, national, global, and planetary. This is Our Story, the one we are born into and the one, while we are alive, that we create.

Our psychological roots come from our parents and our childhoods, just as their psychological roots come from theirs and those of our children will come from ours. Our cultural roots come from centuries of migration and development. Together, these make up our cultural and psychological heritage, two of the biggest factors in our lives and in our sense of self. Our personal and collective past is what gives us depth and dimension.

It is our responsibility to give our children their past so they can shape their future from respect and knowledge rather than out of ignorance. But for them to know and understand their origin we need to know ours. Rediscovering, like the "flooding river," where we come from personally, socially, culturally, and historically prepares us to mother the future with compassion, power, and pride.

In this chapter, we are locating our riverhead for ourselves and our children, telling our stories of childhood, telling the stories of our parents, our grandparents, the legends of our ancestors. In doing so, we root ourselves in our origins and strengthen our sense of self.

1. Locating Ourselves: Born of Our Ancestors

Last night I had a dream. It was a recurring nightmare that I have had since my childhood. In this recurring nightmare, I am always being chased by something horrible. This thing always chases me into a place where I cannot escape. I either plummet to my death or meet the man from down under who unravels my very long and slavish life with him. As I have grown older, I have been able to turn this nightmare into very interesting dreams. Last night was different. This something finally revealed itself. I was being chased by my mother and behind her was my grandmother and behind her my great grandmother, and so it continued on and on, of me being haunted by the spirits of past generations. It was both horrible and powerful. For the first time I was able to look at my pursuer and see that this thing is not as horrible as I had imagined it would be. In fact it was very beautiful. The power of these women from past generations was breathtaking.

—Journey into Motherhood workshop participant, JULIE ANDERSEN

Our world is one of a thousand languages, a thousand cultures, many colors of people and many traditions. Everyone who lives here has come from somewhere else, starting with the American Indians, who came more than ten thousand years ago to the most recent immigrants from Cambodia, Cuba, and El Salvador. Our North American identities are almost always mixed, if not racially, then ethnically. Our society is multicultural even if our homes are not. And even if our parents both come from the same ethnic group and religion, born and raised in the same little town, still their stories part in fascinating ways as they weave back into history.

This section is about connecting with your ancestors. The focus is on your heritage, how you are connected to the world, to history, to cultural traditions. One of the reasons you investigate your heritage and your history is to be able to give it to your children. You remember your own cultural identities and what you are proud of so you can pass on that pride to your children. As well, you are honest about any shame or guilt you may feel about your history or the history of your people. Hidden shame translates into self-hatred, which, on a subconscious level, gets passed on to your children as an unnecessary secret burden or lack of self-esteem.

In doing this writing, you locate yourself in history, along with your child and the father of your child. You locate yourself in a community, in relation rather than in isolation. You learn to see universal connections between all human beings and to celebrate human diversity. Your baby will soon become a member of your tribe as well as a citizen of the planet.

Getting Ready

Imagination is the "flooding" that allows our memory, like the Mississippi River, to return to where it once had been. To prepare for your ancestral journey, close your eyes and imagine being alive at another time in history. Go back as far as you want to. Who might you have been in 50,000 B.C.? 2000 B.C.? in the 1400s? Look at your feet. Are you wearing sandals, bear fur, buckskin boots? What is around you? Describe the landscape you are in, the sounds you hear, what you are wearing, what you are doing, where you are going. Let your fantasy and joy of whimsy have no bounds. If the whole picture does not get clear in your mind's eye, start with one detail and let the other details arise with your words as you are writing.

Journeying

1) By remembering our ancestors and extended families, we locate ourselves and our children in time and space. Draw the family tree of your child. Talk to your partner. Make phone calls to relatives to get more information. Be sure to include at what point each branch came to this country and from where. Next to each name, write a key image you have of them. Example: *My maternal great-grandmother, Bubbe, at ninety, I see her: her full gray hair brightened by the beach light, inviting yet another homeless person to sleep on her sandy threadbare couch.* If you have a photo of the person, place it by their name. You might want to do a small version of the tree in your journal and another one on a larger piece of paper to put up in your house.

2) This is a great time to contact your parents, your grandparents, any living elders of your tribe. Listen to their stories and write them down. They are your stories as well. Strung together, these anecdotes, reminiscences, and tall tales make up your child's family history, a history that will be lost if you don't write it down.

3) Write down the things you are proud of about the cultural and religious traditions of your family. Include what has been passed down to you through your mother, what has been passed down to you through your father, as well as what you have borrowed from elsewhere or created for yourself. Include food, aesthetics, values, art and music, language, spirituality, holidays, any traditions that you can remember. Include what you are proud of about your people's history. These are the aspects of your heritage that you will want to teach your child.

4) Write down any parts of your family history and the history of your people about which you feel shame or guilt. Are there any elements of your

cultural and religious traditions that you don't want to pass on to your child? Why?

Ask the father of your child to do the preceding exercises also. The heritage of your child is from the combination of the two of you. If there is no father present, biology may become less important than guardianship. The identity of your child will be an expression of your combined cultures, traditions, and points of view, not only of the biological mothers and fathers but of the actual parents of the child, the people who raise him day in and day out.

2. When I Was a Child . . .

Would that life were like the shadow cast by a wall or a tree, but it is like the shadow of a bird in flight.

—the Talmud

Childhood is a critical piece of the puzzle, that strange shape that, when you put it down on the table, suddenly makes the whole picture recognizable. Make no bones about it, the source of our adulthood is our childhood.

But you are not just an adult anymore. You are a pregnant adult and there is another "hood" to think about: motherhood, an unwieldy combination of the other two. What does that same childhood you may have had occasion to revisit before mean to you now? Once your childhood simply helped you to understand yourself as an adult. Now your childhood teaches you to be a mother.

When you allow the river of your memories to flood the landscape of your childhood, you resurrect the child's point of view. This time, when you reawaken your childhood with your words, you will not only be locating the source of who you are today and treating yourself to a greater awareness of the woman you have come to be. Now you have a responsibility beyond self-preservation. You are at this very moment growing the person who will be most affected by what you learn from your childhood and who will be, without a doubt, the most appreciative audience of your childhood memoirs anywhere on earth.

In this section, you go back to your childhood to remember what it is to be a child in this world, the delight and the freshness of things, the pain of not understanding, the intensity of emotion, the power and the powerlessness, the play. You will write from a child's voice, reexperiencing the innocence and freedom you felt as a child, reeducating yourself to the unique needs and sensitivities of children. In doing so, you prepare yourself to be a more compassionate mother, a better ally to your child as she grows up.

Getting Ready

Sometimes our earliest memories are the origin of our passions, the things that fascinate us or that we most care about. Close your eyes and let your mind sift back to your earliest years. What astonished you? Our senses are our best guides into our huge stash of memories. Remember a first sound you heard. A first smell or texture. The first time you noticed light. Let your senses take you back to the earliest moment you can remember, and when you get there, write down everything you see, touch, hear, smell, and taste. Write how you feel. Keep going. Write a list of primal fascinations and innocent delights.

> If life has a base that it stands upon, if it is a bowl that one fills and fills and fills—then my bowl without a doubt stands upon this memory. It is of lying half asleep, half awake, in bed in the nursery at St. Ives. It is of hearing the waves breaking, one, two, one, two, and sending a splash of water on the beach; and then breaking one, two, one, two, behind the yellow blind. It is of hearing the blind draw its little acorn across the floor as the wind blew the blind out. It is of

lying and hearing this splash and seeing this light, and feeling, it is almost impossible that I should be here; of feeling the purest ecstasy I
can conceive.

—VIRGINIA WOOLF

Journeying

1) Close your eyes and remember your first home. Whatever house, apartment, trailer, or other place of residence comes to your mind first, go into
that one. Notice how small you are, how old you are, how your head comes
up to the top of the tables or below them. Look at your feet and notice what
shoes you're wearing. Walk through all the rooms slowly at your own pace.
Notice the smells in each room, the way the light sits, the textures, the
sounds, the energy. Pay attention to what object stands out, what you long to
touch, how you feel in each place. Are there people there? Who? What are
they doing? After you have guided yourself through your home, write down
the images. Write in the first person tense from the voice of the child. You
will be amazed by what you can recall. The unconscious selection of sensory
details from our memory contains a map of our emotional life. Through
writing you are grounding yourself in your own reality at the same time you
are rediscovering who you are.

2) You become a child to remember your childhood, the wide eyes, the
sweeping gestures, the uninhibited voice. Close your eyes and remember an
incident that happened to you when you were between two and ten years old.
Your first experience of injustice, your first best friend, your first triumph,
your first betrayal. Something that surprised you or taught you something
new, perhaps one of life's lessons. Maybe you were climbing a fence with
your first "boyfriend" and the picket you were counting on to hold your
weight gave way, or you balanced without training wheels, or your cat ran
away. Imagine yourself at that age, running to your mother to tell her what
happened. Breathless and fast, let it spill out of your mouth in the voice of
the child. Illogical, ungrammatical, with the urgency of innocent communi-

cation. Write "I . . ." Now write another incident, perhaps from a more reflective, adult voice. Keep going. The better you know yourself as a child, the better you will be able to connect with the child you are creating.

Looking at the Map

For the past few weeks, you have been reconstructing the "ancient" past of your child's family history and unearthing your own early memories. By locating yourself in relation to your personal history and ancestral heritage, you give your child the gift of connection to something much larger than herself.

Meanwhile you, the determined trekker through landscapes you may never have imagined even existed, will be justly rewarded for your efforts. Even now, at the end of your first trimester, possibly even before you are rich and famous, you've gotten an enviable head start on your memoirs. You have solidified into a real person who is really pregnant. You can look in the mirror and say in an unquavering voice: "Yes, this is who I am."

You are ready to go on to the next stage of your journey. To continue the process of redefining your identity, you must enter the world of the Mother.

Letter to Your Child

Filled now with your heritage and history, write a letter to your fetus.

> Dear Matagalpa,
> Now you are three months. Your sexuality is forming, they say. And are you North American? You who were conceived in Nicaragua in Central America, you whose architecture is half-Italian, conducted from strains of Mediterranean music blood bones history as well as my own ancestral strains: Scottish, French, British, and Russian Jew. You are in the womb of a U.S. citizen. And are you North Ameri-

can? You belong to no nation at this time. You have no passport. You are a human traveler, wed to no law or culture. You are free of national identity, free of memories of mistreatment, free of guilt. I am white. I am single. I am middle class. I am many things. But you, Matagalpa, are simply human. You could be born anywhere. And are you North American? You do not know the array of names society has already mapped out for you, the pain some of those names could cause you, the privilege some of those names could bring you. You are affected indirectly by those names through your mother. But you yourself are not them. They do not bind you. I want you to remember this moment, Matagalpa. You are a human being. A miracle of hope. Your world perspective is not tainted by division or even difference. You are already the product of human history, of social history, of migrations and wars, of prejudices and inequality, of justice and injustice. Like a built-in kitchen, it comes with the house. But none of this is inside you. None of this takes up space in your memory. None of this is in your heart.

Remember this moment, Matagalpa. The passing of gods.

—*Letters to Matagalpa*

Weeks 1–13

Redefining Ourselves

Your Second Trimester

Weeks 14–27

❧

"I am Mother."

If a woman is shopping for a new outfit that she will wear forever, the smart thing for her to do is to try it on. This is the purpose of the second trimester. Compared to the hormonal/emotional turbulence of the first trimester, the second trimester is a calm sea. The condition of being pregnant and carrying a fetus has shifted from fiction to fact. The threat of miscarriage diminishes. Morning sickness usually passes and there is not as much physical discomfort as in the third trimester, yet birth is not yet frighteningly imminent. With her energy restored and suddenly available for use, a pregnant woman's intuitive tendency is to focus on her most critical relationships: her mother, her father, her partner, her fetus.

In the following three chapters, "Our Mothers," "Redefining Motherhood," and "Inner and Outer Child," we ask ourselves the question: What does it mean to be a mother? We explore the meaning of our new identity, the one we are not identified with yet. We go into the fitting room and try on the mother outfit our own mothers wore to see how it fits. We try on our grandmother's outfit. We try on different cultural models, different historical models, different advertising models until the fitting room looks like a garage sale of old clothes. As we try on all these outfits, we stay alert, always noticing where each one fits and where it doesn't, building for ourselves a stockpile of critical information and insight. Then we are ready to start making our mother outfit from scratch, selecting our own fabric and cutting it out on the table. We design it how we want it to feel and look and sew our own outfit per our own instructions. Through this shopping, we learn to forgive our own mothers and experience more compassion for all mothers. We are wise women writing ourselves into our future.

During the second trimester, we are changed forever by the deep physical sensation of holding life inside us for the first time. We are shifting from being our mother's daughter to being a mother ourselves. Affirming this process of separation from our own mother, we begin the process of separation with our own child. We hear the fetal heartbeat and feel our own baby moving. The doors have opened wider and prenatal bonding can begin to flourish. Communication with the spirit inside us starts to be real. It comes like a revelation: We are not one but two.

We are mothers.

Four

Our Mothers

Your Fourth Month

She is confetti,

glittering everywhere at once.

Her hair flashes, mirrors

caught by lightning as she soars,

a silver bird.

She is power lines sizzling and buzzing

then her sparks fly,

ignite a fire of her intellect

burning the land, purifying

a fire spanning continents

jumping oceans

the tentacles of her brain

flow out the flames of her hair

to make the stars sparkle,

the sun burn.

In her bosom burns a hearth

rounded in marble

with blue-grey veins running through,

always coursing with the blood

of affection, fierce protection

her passionate flames licking clean her marble teeth

which can flash a sunbeam

or turn on you

gleaming wolves in the moonlight.

—"Tora," by writing workshop participant, KARRA BIKSON

During your first trimester, you unraveled your destiny, remembered the wisdom of your body, embraced your joy, your fears, your ambivalence, and were "born again." So what could possibly get in your way of a perfect birth?

You guessed it! Your *mother.* That most maligned of human creatures the likes of which you are about to become.

On the deepest level, your definition of being a mother comes from your experience of your own mother. She is your encyclopedia for the meaning of that ancient word, minute by minute, page by page, with lots of illustrations, starting in the womb. A first look, a touch, a song, yelling, abuse, love, endless incidents that, combined, give you your personal understanding of what it means to be a mother.

However she did her work (a profession for which she, too, was never trained except unwittingly by her own mother), your mother was your first teacher.

The equation seems to go like this: "My mother = Mother. I am becoming a Mother. Therefore, I am becoming my mother." It doesn't have to be this way.

Here are three good reasons why I am asking you to take on the momentous task of coming to terms with your mother now during your journey into motherhood.

Number one is this: There is no more important person in your life than your mother, whether you are embracing or rejecting her, in healthy relationship or unhealthy reaction to her, whether she is alive or dead.

Number two is this: If you're not vigilant, you will become her, whether you want to or not. Unconsciously, we repeat our first relationship.

And number three is this: She will soon be your baby's grandmother.

There is no better time than now, when you are becoming a mother, to know your own mother, to understand her, to celebrate and forgive her. As you journey into motherhood, you have the perfect opportunity to define for yourself the kind of mother you want to become and to envision the kind of relationship you want to have with your own child. At the same time, you have the perfect opportunity to transform your relationship with your mother, and to create the relationship with her that you truly want.

Facing and having compassion for the inadequacies of your parents as well as recognizing the good they've given you prepares you for the inevitable pleasures and disappointments of your new family. It is easy to blame your mother. It is not as easy to forgive her. Yet forgiveness is an important part of the process of reconstructing a positive relationship with her. Through writing clear affirmations, you commit to being both the mother and the daughter you want to be.

1. Locating Ourselves: In Her Shoes

So who is this woman you call mother? In my creative writing classes I ask my students to write from the perspective of someone they have very strong feelings about, to become that person. There is no better way to understand and develop a fictional character than to imagine being that person and to write from his or her voice. The same is true of understanding real people. Except that it is harder because there is more at stake.

It takes courage to become someone else. You have to let go of yourself. You have to cross the line into forbidden territory and trust what you find there. Once you cross that threshold out of yourself and really get into someone else's shoes—feel their sweat, their heartbeat, their bones, their rhythms—anything can happen. You don't have to think. The voice of the person you have become takes hold and gains momentum. You have actually entered another world, the inexhaustibly rich world of the imagination.

One of my workshop participants who was adopted while still a baby did some writing exercises in which she crossed the line into what had felt like forbidden territory to her: she got into the shoes of her birth mother. She began to discover things that became very important to her. But she couldn't get very far. Her birth mother, whom she had met, gave her too little information. She decided to write a book, autobiographical-fiction, in which she created her mother's entire life from the bits she knew, what she intuited, and what she simply made up.

I don't believe there is ever really anything that is absolutely made up. Even in whimsy, there is reason. When you remember your mother and when you imagine being your mother, trust what comes to you. What few people realize is that our imaginations tell the truth. Not always the scientific, measurable kind of truth but something beyond that. Something of great significance.

Getting Ready

Get out photos of your mother at different ages, with you and without you. Sit with them. Put key photos or copies of them in your journal. Take your time. The photos will help transport your mother into your personal sphere at the same time they take you back to who she was at different times and bring up memories of your relationship. If you have no photos or few of them, ask for them from those who do or just use your imagination.

Start out by remembering your life with your mother, the period of time you lived with her. Close your eyes and start from the beginning. Watch the moments go by on the movie screen in your mind. Read the exercise you did from an infant's point of view in Chapter Two in the section called "Birth." Was your mother there? What did you remember? How did you feel with her as a baby? Go through the years. Remember incidents—the ecstatic, the joyous, the shaming or humiliating, the violent, the angry, the fun. Watch the scenes go by. Pick out the squares of celluloid and write them down, image after image, the favorite times, the least favorite times. Start with the earliest memories. Then write them down as they come to you, in any order. Use sensory detail. Smells, colors, textures, light, sound, taste, visual detail. Example: 1)*While I lie mute, a thermometer plugging my speech, my mother sits across from me on her giant bed teaching me sign language so I can speak to her. 2) My mother braiding my hair in the bright light over her bathroom sink when she was angry or in a hurry, pulling the strands hard as she threaded them one over the other, one over the other, my tears falling into the cold sink making her braid harder and faster, my scalp stretched like the skin of a drum.*

Once you're done, select two of these images and take it further. One favorite and one least favorite moment. Write each one as a scene, a page or two. All the details. What were you wearing? What was she wearing? Describe the surroundings, the air, the light.

Journeying

1) Now your memory is stimulated, lubricated like an old engine. Let's try driving it down the road. In the first chapter, you wrote the crossroads in your life that brought you to the cusp of motherhood, perhaps for the first time. Now it is time for you to write the stepping-stones of your mother's life, the major moments after which everything changed, internally, externally, or both. Think of all the pain she has experienced, the revelations, the discouragement, the victories. Think of all her memories, what she has done. Write ten stepping-stones. At first ten may seem like a lot. Maybe you feel you know very little about your mother's life. Once you start, you will discover you know more than you thought. Become her. Write in her voice in the first person in whatever order it comes to you. The voice will carry you forward. Don't think. Allow the voice, the words, the rhythms of speech to arise within you. Describe the incident and express your mother's feelings

from her point of view. Imagine that she is talking to someone in particular, a stranger. Someone on the bus. Someone she sat next to on a park bench. Someone who will just listen and not judge her. Write for twenty minutes.

2) No doubt your relationship with your mother is complex, with so many facets and aspects to it that it would be impossible to describe it in a few words. Yet that is what I am asking you to do. Cut through the layers. Have you ever opened up a golf ball? Inside the serene white wrapping there are a million small rubber bands. They seem to be tangled together endlessly, irrevocably. Yet they unravel easily and in the middle is the essence of the golf ball, the gold itself, the inner hole in one. Write the essence of your relationship with your mother. State the heart of the matter concisely. Write for five to ten minutes.

> Dependent. I am her reluctant confidante, the one she can trust with her secrets and bad news. The one she tells things that she has no one else to tell. And though I tell her little, I rely on her reliance. I feel like her protector and that makes me feel strong in the world.
>
> —Journey into Motherhood workshop participant, LINDA DALLIN

> Like wood. With distance and caution and stiff cordiality. "Thank you for calling," like a receptionist. Bricks stacked between us. The strain of wanting to please the other and it's always, always impossible. I'll always be too fat; she'll always be too—what? Too her. Picking, fussing. Moping. Complaining. Critical. Our relationship is not real. Not open. We don't tell each other our worries, or our joys. Just the facts, ma'am.
>
> —Journey into Motherhood workshop participant, SUSAN ITO

3) Write a dialogue with your mother. A dialogue is a mutual meeting of persons, each accepting, speaking to, and most important, listening to the

other. This dialogue enables you to reenter your relationship with your mother from an interior point of view. Have the conversation you always meant to have. Say directly what you have been wanting to say. Allow her to speak frankly. After you write your part, stop a minute. Close your eyes. Actually listen to what she has to say, then write it down.

2. Sifting for Gold

Between 1845 and 1848, during the peak of the gold rush in California, hundreds of people, mostly men, went in search of gold and came back rich with it. After that things seemed to dry up. People straggled into the mother lode but came back empty-handed. I went with my son when he was three years old to Jamestown in the Sierras. Jamestown is a town that has been restored to look just as it did in the gold rush days: stores glittering with homemade candy, the dusty main street empty of cars, but filled, instead, with the clip-clop of horses' hooves and bandits robbing your stage coach. There, for a small fee, you can still pan for gold—which we did. Sifting through the detritus, we could both just barely make out a few flecks of gold. My son was very excited. Even gold dust shines in the sun, delighting the eye. Mother Earth is abundant with gold and other beautiful minerals yet we rarely look for it and when we do look, we rarely find it.

It is the same with your own mothers. Most of us experienced a gold rush in our relationship with our mothers. It probably lasted a few years, just like the California gold rush, maybe the first two or three years of your life, maybe a little more, or less. In those first days with her, she was home, gold, milk, life, primordial love. But since then, how often have you gone back to pan for gold in your mother lode? Your principal source?

Now that you've done the exercises in the last section, remembering your mother and getting inside of her life, you may have noticed jewels you had been unaware of before. Perhaps you feel more compassion for her, just as you would for any human being to whom you truly pay attention. Just as you may feel more compassion for yourself as you move through each chapter of this book, stopping to pay attention to yourself, looking and listening to who you are, taking stock of yourself at this point in your evolution. Compassion breeds compassion. The more compassion you unearth for your mother and yourself, the more you will find available for your child. You are like three trees standing against a twilight sky, all changing in the descending light.

How often do you praise your mother? How often do you tell her, or yourself, what specifically she has given you that you are thankful for?

You are becoming a mother yourself. You too will be blamed or forgiven. But will you be praised?

One way to start the momentum of mother appreciation from the child you are giving birth to is to begin appreciating your own mother now, sifting for gold and writing it down. What richer place is there for you to start defining motherhood for yourself than by identifying the very things you loved about your own mother's parenting and choosing to repeat what works?

Getting Ready

Imagine a fantasy mother, the mother you wish your mother had been. Don't be reasonable. Exaggerate. If it crosses your mind that you're asking for too much, dash the thought. What does she look like? What does she wear? How does she talk? What does she love? How does she treat you? What does she give you? How does she respond to you?

Journeying

1) To be the mother you wish your mother had been, you first need to locate what you received from her, what you missed, what needs you felt weren't met, what she actually did and didn't do. Then you can see clearly and specifically how you want to be, decide to be that way, and do your best to put this into practice when you've got your child in tow.

Take a few moments to brag about your mother. What did you love about her? What are the specific things your mother did, specific things she said, and specific ways she was that you want to repeat? This list will be one of the most important writings for you to keep at easy reach once your baby is born.

2) My son, at two years old, informed me that he loved and hated me. At five, he reminded me that sometimes I am nice and sometimes I am mean, that sometimes he likes me and sometimes he doesn't. When he is angry with me, he wants to "kill" me. He wants to kill the bad witch. Write down all the things you hate, or that simply annoy you about your mother, all the things you don't want to repeat. Go back to the beginning.

> My mother always put her fingers on my face to change it. Stretching out frown lines, moving hair, wiping off sand, always without asking, and usually when I was talking to her about something else. The result: I didn't feel like she was listening to me or that what I had to say and felt was important. I learned to distrust her love for me; she didn't seem able to simply love me as I was, unconditionally.
>
> —the author's journal

3. Agent for Change: Becoming the Mother You Intend to Be

For women who have every intention of mothering differently than their own mothers, one of the most frustrating things about bringing up their own children is finding themselves repeating the same old things. Mothering is a job we have never been taught to do and so, through default, we repeat what we experienced, we repeat what we observed, particularly under stress. It is like an inner program we often feel helpless to shut off.

This is your responsibility. Not your child's. How are you going to be different? You are not trying to be the perfect mother. You will make mistakes. You will raise your voice. You will say something that later you wish you had never said. You will be the witch that poisons the apple. At least once.

It takes a terrific imagination, cleaned of the aggressive programming of the past, to see that anything else is even possible. Every person has a massive resistance to change and it is that resistance that we first need to break through. Nicaraguan poet Giocanda Belli wrote during the Sandinista-Contra War, "Sometimes I think it's easier to face an enemy army in combat than to confront the inheritance of concepts and prejudices we carry inside ourselves and to transform it." How do we cut through resistance? By starting—even with the smallest thing—and changing it. Then going on to the next thing. Until the knowledge grows in you that you are an agent for change, that you can change anything you set your mind to change, including your own prejudices, your own behavior.

Getting Ready

Some of you may feel as though you have never changed anything. Sometimes all it takes is *remembering* to put you back in touch with your own transformative power, the root of hope, vision, and strategy. When you write, you remember. You remember the first thing and that opens the door to the next memory, and so on. Sometimes big doors fly open wide and lots of memories come into consciousness. Take time now to write down things you have changed in your own life. Small things. Big things. A habit, a pattern, a time you broke away from something that started feeling programmed and did something different, when you facilitated change in someone else or in your community. Notice that nothing has control over you but yourself. You are completely responsible for your own changes. Each time you change, you have made a choice. At the top of the page write, "I am an agent for change." Then write for twenty minutes or more.

Journeying

1) Go back to "Sifting for Gold" and read what you wrote in the second writing exercise, the things your mother did that you don't want to repeat. Write

the essence of each one of them and then, next to it, write what you will do differently in each case. Write your goal in the present tense as if it were already happening now.

> Memory: My mother was not physically affectionate with me. Goal: I often touch my child and link with him physically. I do this naturally without making a big deal out of it. I respond positively to his affection toward me and always return it.
>
> —the author's journal

2) You are doing a wonderful job of envisioning the kind of mother you want to be. You have an excellent foundation. You have located the things your mother taught you that you want to use and the things she taught you that you have chosen to unlearn. You have seen what you want to replace this with, how you will be different. These are the things that are deep inside you, that hold the most emotional weight. Now, build on this foundation.

What are other ways of being, other behaviors and actions you will take with your child that you never experienced yourself? These may be things you heard someone else say, things you read about, things you make up. Until I heard another pregnant woman tell me about the way her mother tacked up huge pieces of paper on the walls of her living room for her children to paint on, I had never even imagined such a mother or that such fun at home could be possible. I started to think of other wacky things to do in which the goal was fun and fun alone.

> We had just moved to a new house. After removing all the dishes and breakables from the cardboard boxes, there was a mountain of wrinkled up newspaper to gather and put in the recycling bin. Instead, we spread them all over our new living room a foot high, rolled them into balls and had a fight, diving into the paper, laughing hysterically, gathering huge bunches of newspaper balls as fast as we could and throwing them all at once at the other person. I swallowed my do-

mestic pride in neatness and we left them there for four days and every day we whooped it up and played.

—the author's journal

3) Go back and read everything you have written about your mother. Notice how you defined your relationship. Pregnancy and early motherhood is an opportune time to change the relationship you have with your mother for the better. The section entitled "In Her Shoes" gave you a chance to write down what the essence of your relationship with your mother has been. Envision the relationship you want to have with your mother now. What is its essence? Start by writing down the three key things you feel are lacking in your relationship. Then write down how it will be different, as affirmations, as if it were already happening now. One of the best ways to affect change in a relationship (or yourself) is to act as if the thing had already changed. You live *in* your goal, not outside it. You become it. A goal is a way of being. Example: *My mother trusts that I can take care of myself.*

What is one way you will be different with your mother? Example: *When my mother does or says something that angers or irritates me, I will not respond as I always did (my knee-jerk reaction of expressing my accumulated anger). Instead I will hug her and tell her I love her right in that moment.*

One thing is your intention to be different. Another is actually to do something about it. What is an action you will take? Small or big. By when will you do it? What is the next action you will take? Example: *I will send a letter to my mother telling her what I love about her and her parenting by the end of next week.*

Looking at the Map

Your relationship to your mother and to your child will evolve as the years go by. Your close ties to your baby will continue to evoke memories of how it felt to be connected to your own mother. Keep writing about your feelings as your child grows. Continue to write honestly, without fear, communicating with yourself, clarifying, and letting go, as an actively parenting mother year after year.

And remember, when your real baby is on the scene, it is easy to forget the work you have been doing during your "enlightened" pregnancy. Use this journal as a tool. Remember to come back to the writings you are doing now. Let them continue to be your guides.

Beyond Our Mothers

All of the exercises in this chapter are relevant for anyone else other than your mother or in addition to your mother who raised you: father, grandmother, second mother, aunt. Complete the above exercises with this person (or people) as the subject.

Get into your father's shoes. Sift for gold. See what he did that you don't want to repeat and what he did that you do want to repeat. Write about a fantasy father. If the father of your child is involved in the birth and will be involved in parenting your child, ask him to do these exercises also. Include the person or people who will be sharing parenting with you in the process you are going through.

Note: If you are planning to have a prenatal diagnosis to test for any possible abnormalities in your fetus, the third and fourth months are usually when you will do it. Please go to Chapter Six, Section 1, "I Can Feel the Baby," exercise 3, for a writing exercise that will help you through the range of emotions connected with this experience.

Letter to Your Child

Write a letter to your fetus and sign it "mother."

Dear you, crystallizing dream,
How big are you? How does it feel in there? You are almost big enough to reach me—to push your sensation out to my rim. Will I believe you then, I wonder?

You can't feel how much I have imagined you—inside me like this and out in the world when you finally come to join us. I want so much to see who you are—take you on walks, giggle, muse, make music. I imagine that you will sing and find your own poetry to teach me, your own movements to carve the day.

I trust this magic, this timing—even the distance between us. You are my pit taking form, my fruit ripening into something amazing I cannot yet know. I am your trusty tree, protector, wind chime, odometer. We will join forces at our own perfect pace.

—Journey into Motherhood workshop participant, HELEN COHEN

Five

Redefining Motherhood

Your Fifth Month

It was as Mother that woman was fearsome: it is in maternity that she must be transfigured and enslaved.

—SIMONE DE BEAUVOIR

Each society from every age has defined the meaning of motherhood in its own terms and, as a result, has imposed its own restrictions and expectations on mothers.

In ancient times, women were worshiped for their childbearing powers. In the Middle Ages of Europe as well as in agricultural and preindustrial societies everywhere, the family was a unit of production and reproduction rather than emotional satisfaction. Mothers were important not just because they raised children with the values of their communities but because they produced workers and heirs to property. In late nineteenth-century Europe and North America, motherhood became an idealized concept with religious and moral overtones: "the destiny of the redeemed world is put into your hands." Today, in Western society, motherhood is in crisis. It is no longer assumed to be the primary purpose of a woman's life. It has become a subject full of difficulty, uncertainty, and paradox. The meaning of motherhood has become plagued with contradiction, illusion, and confusion.

Not only do we mothers and mothers-to-be have to wade through a history of sexist ideology about motherhood, mother-child relationships, and women in general, but we also need to sift through the often contradictory voices among feminists as well as between feminists and more traditional women about the meaning of being a mother in today's world. There are historical reasons for our feelings of ambivalence about embracing motherhood. Motherhood is personal and it is also political.

As we spin into the third millennium, the world continues to change rapidly with its corresponding impact on the configuration of the family and the meaning of motherhood. One thing is certain. Motherhood is no longer an automatic thing, part of being grown-up and doing what is expected in the world. And so we are faced with a question: How do we make rocking the cradle be, as well as feel, honorable and important?

This chapter will help you to answer this question for yourself. You will have the opportunity to discover the origin of any myths, stereotypes, and prejudices about motherhood that you consciously or unconsciously carry inside you. You will explore your own values and beliefs as a foundation for defining motherhood for yourself. And, finally, you will have a chance to be the architect of a new vision, to design a society in which motherhood flourishes and the needs of mothers and children are easily met.

Remember, you are not only pregnant with child. You are pregnant with motherhood, your new role in the world growing inside you.

1. The Mythic Mother

The mythic mother is everything but real. Whether she is idealized or trivialized, heroic or victimized, she is an idea without a heartbeat. The supermom with the superjob, superclean house, superkids. The frigid, unsexy, matronly caretaker. The fertility goddess. The woman in the shoe with so many kids she doesn't know what to do. The earth mother. The witch. Myths and stereotypes are bigger than life. And usually one-sided. One aspect of reality is taken to excess and regarded as the whole—thus becoming caricature, lacking the complexity of what is real.

Yet ideas are powerful. We internalize them as real and often forget that someone actually made them up.

For example: I inherited the stereotype that mothers are boring. I became a mother. Therefore, I decided, I must be boring. I proved this to myself daily by concentrating on everything that was boring about being a mother and ultimately got stuck in the boredom I believed to be inherent in motherhood. However, once I recognized this and acknowledged that boredom is in fact a danger in motherhood, I was able to choose to make it interesting. I need to remind myself every day. Reinventing motherhood takes vigilance. I redefine motherhood as stimulating and become more fascinating myself.

In this section, you will come to understand how prejudice works and see ways that you internalize these judgments unconsciously and act on them as if they were true. You will put your cards on the table for all to see. You will excavate your mental files for the ideas of motherhood you have inherited and the ones you have accrued over the years like dust. By clarifying what your ideas about motherhood are, you bring them into consciousness, then you can hold them up to the light of scrutiny. Once you recognize and admit to the ideas you currently carry inside you, you can begin the process of authentic self-definition.

Journeying

1) What are the notions you carry inside you about the meaning of motherhood that came to you from society, advertising, and your cultural heritage? Listen to the voices. Write down the myths and stereotypes you have accumulated over time. If you are aware of where a stereotype came from, write that down, too.

2) Read over your list of opinions from the last exercise, a kind of map of your mind. Have your ideas about motherhood shifted over time? What has changed your understanding of the concept? What has had the biggest influence on you? You may feel uncomfortable admitting to your stereotypes and writing them down. Let me tell you, it is well worth it. When you are aware of ways your mind has been manipulated and to what influences you tend to succumb, you free yourself to recover and develop your own values and beliefs.

2. *Reinventing Motherhood*

All concepts are invented. Through the use of our imagination, ingenious thinking, and experiment, they come into being for the first time. They are only relevant, however, to the degree that they are useful. You want your concept of motherhood to be relevant to you, to address your own experience. Yet you are not only reinventing motherhood for yourself. The issues of motherhood touch the lives of three billion mothers today and billions more to come.

The concept of motherhood has been invented and reinvented more than once throughout history. In this section, you will take on the task once again. In the process of clarifying what you want mothering to mean, you will also rediscover what you believe in and reaffirm what has value to you. In doing this, you will not be alone. Millions of mothers want what you want. You will design a blueprint of a world in which your role as a mother has dignity and greatness, a society in which the value of motherhood is made manifest through public support for the needs of all mothers and their children. You are building a foundation for what you want to pass on to your children. You are, after all, their first teacher.

Getting Ready

In 1990, I started putting "mother" down on my job résumé under "special skills" because what I knew as a new mother and what I had already accomplished in just three years of motherhood made me the top candidate for any job. This is one simple action I continue to take that challenges my employers to redefine the meaning of motherhood. A mother is a professional. She is a white collar worker and she is a blue collar worker. The surgeon and the janitor. The executive director and the construction worker. The teacher and the mechanic. I have grown to be proud of my identity as a mother. I am the bearer of the miracle of human life. I am unlimited and capable of doing anything. And so are you. Write down what skills you imagine it takes to nurture a child well; what character attributes it requires. Include everything. Be careful not to minimize any aspect of this work or to leave anything out. Spell it out clearly and completely. You will end up with a monumental job description. Later, when your baby is born, add and amend the job description as needed. But always come back to it. Put a copy of it up on your refrigerator to remind yourself (and others) of the value, range, and sophistication of your labor-intensive work.

Journeying

1) Being aware of which of your values, and resultant choices, are going to be supported by society, your government, your religious institution, your cultural community, the general population, or even your family and friends, and which values, and resultant choices, may, on the other hand, be controversial, deemed unimportant, or even condemned by these same groupings, will help you in two significant ways. First, you will determine where, as a mother, you can go for support. And second, you will recognize in which areas you are going to have to build strength and alliances to maintain and act on your values. Every mother needs an ally. Discuss all these issues with your partner, a prime potential ally for your parenting. Talk with other pregnant women and new mothers. Build a network of support for your vision of motherhood now, before the baby comes, when you have more time to socialize and think.

What aspects of motherhood that you value privately do you feel are valued publicly? By whom?

What aspects of motherhood that you value privately may be controversial? To whom can you go for support?

2) Envision a society where mothering is valued. Schools, institutions, maternity leave, the workplace, child care, gadgets and accessories in public places to ease the work, advertising, entertainment, culture, family structure,

you name it. Disregard your cynicism for a moment, or any hopelessness. Believe, instead, that anything is possible. This is a society we can create together by seeing it, writing it, and speaking it. Describe what this society would look like.

Looking at the Map

Take a deep breath. You thought you were just having a baby and here you are wrestling with that amorphous fluctuating and powerful idea called motherhood: tackling history, social values, sexism, marketing, and emotional memories of what you've learned from your own mother. Consciousness raising is a tiresome business. It is not, however, without its rewards.

By actually looking at everything that has been planted in your garden, naming what you want and what you don't want to keep, and then planting the seeds you want to see grow and flower in your own and your child's future, you gain self-confidence as you begin to claim your new mother identity. In taking the time to redefine motherhood, you choose not to be a victim of old ideas that offend you or simply don't fit who you are and your vision of life on this planet. You take leadership in your life and provide a model of courage to your children as you thoughtfully discover a satisfying balance between creative self-definition and the wisdom of tradition.

Letter to Your Child

Write a letter to your fetus from your newly developed point of view.

Six

Inner and Outer Child

Your Sixth Month

Listen.

I will do anything:

eat two raw eggs

walk slowly under you

lie on my left side

fall into the juniper bush in the dark

give up

my ankles to salt,

men's desire,

even, at last, my own

I efface

become nothing

a waiting

a moving container

clotted with love.

So that your passage through me
will leave me hollow and confused
directionless, you having gone,

and having come,
who will you be
with your mercury eyes
pink hands flexing
unfathomable needs?

Will I know you then?
For whom shall I have bent
for whose head in my hand
hungered?

—GAIL RUDD ENTREKIN, "This Time"

We're following the yellow brick road. Yet no one has built this road for us. The words we write are the bricks we place one after another to form our own path into the land of motherhood. Along the way, the landscape of our unconscious, most of which has remained a blur for a long time, is finding its shapes and colors. Our lifescapes emerge as if by magic into visibility. We have been venturing into realms of family psychology, family trees, politics, and the intellect in the pursuit of understanding our new role in the world at this time in history. Meanwhile, while we were wandering into our pasts and restructuring paradigms of thinking, *you* were becoming pregnant beyond words.

Look at your belly. You have no waist! You may not have accepted the reality of your fetus before but for the past two months the proof has been overwhelming. To you. To your partner. To the world! If you haven't been wearing extra-large T-shirts, you are probably heavily into maternity fashions, new or used. Bosoms like casava melons, the nipples almost blinking their red neon. You are all curves and fullness and ripeness. Your eroticism is likely to be at high pitch.

Meanwhile, Western medicine, anxious for your fetus to be a Hollywood star, has given her a microphone to sing her heart out and has even given her a debut on the screen. When you heard the rhythm of the fetal heartbeat go *whoosh-whoosh* and saw the tiny arms and legs feathering on a sonogram, how could you not believe? And if, still, you were skeptical, suspicious of Spielberg-like sound and visual effects, what about the overwhelming experience of quickening, that odd sensation of something moving inside your own burgeoning belly? It is your baby, soon to be the big screen star of your life, giving you special bulletins: "I am here," she is saying in her own inimitable way. "By golly, I am here!"

If the child inside you is real, that means the child will really be outside you. And if the child will really be outside you, that means the child really has to come out of you. This knowledge comes to you in fragmentary revelations. As you get closer to your destination, all of your fears, anxieties, doubts, concerns, and questions start to take clearer shapes, sharpening like knives on sandstone.

In the next section, entitled "I Can Feel the Baby!" you will take the time to focus in on your inner child. Not the psychological inner child, the little you that has become so popular and demanding of attention in recent years, but the *real* child inside you. You will talk to her, listen to him, draw him, consider the ramifications of knowing her sex. With your letters you have been cultivating prenatal bonding with your child for over five months. Now your fetus actually has ears to listen. Your relationship with your child can go to a whole new level. Now you can sing, chant, play music, speak to your baby. You can physically respond to his movements and actually interact.

Given that this life inside you will actually have a body out of your womb taking up space in your house, the section called "Now That It's Real, How Do I Take Care of It?" helps you to give authenticity to your outer child. You will imagine holding your baby in your arms, whine to your heart's delight, and contemplate your feelings about shopping for your baby's arrival. These exercises will reveal more than you might think about how you are responding emotionally to the prospect of giving birth and having a fat cheek to kiss.

The section called "Surrender" focuses on the birth itself arising out of the horizon like a sun so all-pervasive in its brightness that you feel overwhelmed by it. Your fears and anxieties about labor and birth are no longer shadows in your backyard. They're sitting right there on your living room couch! And not only that, all your other fears and anxieties about life after birth are sitting there with them, laughing, pouting, and schmoozing as if there were no tomorrow. Dreams about birth may become more nightmarish, reflecting your growing anxiety. Your writing will help you practice for birth by bringing these fears to the surface.

1. "I Can Feel the Baby!"

My baby quivers inside my belly

and my world stops.

Around me, clouded and fuzzy,

typewriters whir,

errand boys run,

telephones ring.

Hustling and bustling, the office carries on.

But I sit, seat pushed back from my desk

with my hand on the future.

—MARLENE ANNE BUMGARNER, "Creation"

When I first felt my baby inside me, my first inclination was to rock. So I did. I got a rocking chair and put it in the back room facing the treetops and scraps of sky where I could hear the aviary sounds of twilight—a thousand birds speaking at once. Suddenly, I had company. My private guest. And I became the respectful host, smiling in my secret knowledge. If I could have hung out fresh towels or put flowers in the guest room, I would have. What I *could* do for my unusual guest was to comfort him by rocking and finally to introduce myself by talking out loud. In addition to my silent written letters and my faith in our telepathic communications, now, I knew, he could hear my voice. I am the only person in the world with this voice and I knew he would remember it.

You are now constantly reminded that there is someone else inside you. Rocking in your rocking chair with your hands spread across the emerging beach ball of your stomach, imagine your child inside you. Imagine the secret life of your unborn child. The reassuring rhythm of your heartbeat is one of the major constellations of her universe. He falls asleep to it, wakes to it, moves to it, rests to it. A pregnant abdomen and uterus is a very noisy place and your fetus is listening to everything. She hears the rumblings in your stomach like gentle thunder in a stormy sky. The heartbeat is her single constant. Now she hears voices, quiet but audible. Yours especially.

You probably have a few long months ahead of you before your sensitive guest will be in your hands, yet you can begin now, from the very edge of consciousness onward, to let your child know she is wanted and loved. You can communicate with your fetus now. Studies show that there are traces of memory in a human being starting from the fifth or sixth month of being in the womb.

Getting Ready

The feeling of having two people in one body can be surreal or harmonious or existentially threatening. Close your eyes, hold your hands over your belly, and imagine your fetus-child curled up and alert in your womb. Write without thinking about how you feel having this human being growing inside you. Do you feel exuberant, tender, confused, violated? Do you experience your fluttering fetus as a welcome guest or an intruder? Your feelings and fantasies are multiple and complex. Don't hold back. What does the feeling of having this life inside you remind you of? Don't clam up because suddenly you're aware your fetus may be listening. Your honesty will pay off. You increase your potential for loving your child well by loving yourself well. To love yourself well you need to pay attention to and be honest about your feelings. When you are done writing, close your eyes again and picture your fetus-child. Now draw the image you just saw in your mind's eye. Your right brain is a wellspring of symbols, the stuff of your dreams. What do you see? A rubber doorstop, a bird, a scientific rendering of a fetus? Or maybe just a circle, pure and simple?

> Mossy rock, tree limb, foot of a rabbit, large edible root, serpent lashing from side to side, a cushion, veiled lamp, some-kind-of-movable-parts-doll-deity, sponge, rising loaf, butterfly, trapped bird, wax, mold, flame, a small man writing, small woman eating & lifting elbow, a bat, succulent plant, something in the oven, a potato doll, a doll of seashells, sandbag, large fish swimming in circles, a clock, something silent, a silent toy car, a memory, coiled & striking, fish hidden behind rock, every color & no color, a telephone receiver, submarine, rubber expanding, held together with rubber bands, labial, fingers playing an instrument, inflatable doll, a school of dolphins, tidal wave, unease, planet with circling rings, not made in a lab, a thunder storm, lashing out, a chest of toys, sedentary monkey, jack-in-the-box, icebox, lamps going on, a solar system, a tiny city ruled by a cobra, a city of clam inhabitants, an excursion, a place with hats on, an owl, a bear in a cave, drifting raft, boat on the waves, electricity, dancing flame's shadow on your face, bulging package, a rushed person gesturing excitedly as in hailing a speeding taxi cab, quicksilver.
>
> —ANNE WALDMAN, "Enceinte"

Journeying

1) Write how you felt when you had your first ultrasound and saw your fetus for the first time. I know pregnant women who have carried their ultrasound photos of their fetus in their wallets to show off to friends. Nevertheless, this is a photo of your child, your inner child, the mystery that has not been solved.

I enter Nuclear Medicine like a child, holding my bladder between my legs with all my might without inhibition. The advice nurse has instructed me to drink four quarts of water before coming and not to pee so that their machines can find you. I enter lopsided like a drowning yacht. They make me wait past my appointment time. I look at the other pregnant women in the waiting room and wonder how they manage to read magazines and smile. I am afraid something is just about to leak onto my gaudy orange institutional chair when they call my name. . . .

They lay us down and look at you with sound. They count your rings as if you were a felled tree. I see your feathery presence out of the corner of my eye.

. . . I feel comforted. I know you. I have spoken to you. I smile with my secret knowledge. By the looks of you, you are a decade away from ever sitting in a high chair. You are a dream suddenly made concrete by a thousand dots that aren't really you but that look like you. . . . You do not charm me. You do not attract me. You are that very shimmering I spoke to last week. I am amazed. You are the oddest bedfellow I have ever had. When they turn you off, I feel you are really gone.

—*Letters to Matagalpa*

2) Gender is a big deal. Just ponder, for a moment, how men are treated in the world, how women are treated, how the norms are changing. Think about how boys are treated and how girls are treated: by fathers, by mothers, by schoolteachers, by advertisers. Notice what has been expected of boys versus girls and vice versa. Think about your own struggle to be respected as a complete human being and to assume your rights rather than fighting for them on all occasions and in all places. Take this opportunity to focus in on your feelings about the gender of your newborn. What are your ideas about boys? About girls? Do you want a girl or a boy? How do you think it will make a difference? Maybe you don't care, you are so pleased to be creating a child at all. Still, the moment your baby is born, your ideas about gender will

come into play fast and furiously without your even realizing it. These ideas affect your expectations of your child, the way you talk to her, dress him, treat her. All of which affects the way your child will behave in the world, what he expects from himself as a boy or herself as a girl. These are difficult questions. Do you want to lay the foundation in your child for a liberated woman or man? What does that mean to you? Gender conditioning is powerful and goes into operation immediately, if not from us, from the world around us. Because of modern technology you have the choice of knowing the sex of your child before he or she becomes an outer child. If you have already found out the sex during a sonogram, write down your reaction to this knowledge. If you don't know yet, use your words to reflect upon this archetypal topic so that you are a more conscious parent when the baby arrives.

Deadpan and with a tad of mischievousness, the bald doctor suddenly swings slightly on his stool like monkey see, monkey do and sings to me, "I know what sex it is."

Sex?

What chapter is this? The climax before the first page? The conclusion before the climax? I am not ready for this. I just haven't thought about it much at your age. You are simply Matagalpa. My fetus. Sex has nothing to do with it. Fetuses are scientific objects after all, not genders.

Nothing in my little mirror image of you gives me a clue. How does he know? Perhaps only he can interpret anything out of a low-resolution scan of sound waves. I glance up to my left. The mouths of my two bodyguards, my brother and a friend, are agape. Out of ignorance or wisdom, I cannot determine which. Still, the fascination on their buffoon faces tempts me to know the truth.

As my mouth mouths the words, "What sex is it?" time slows down. The fast-paced Hollywood hospital scene suddenly goes slack. The supporting actors are gone or invisible or suddenly undramatic. I don't notice them. Like a criminal in court waiting for the judge to give the jury's sentence, everything past and future funnels into the black hole of the present and disappears. There are only two choices flashing like neon on Las Vegas night clubs. *Girl. Boy. Girl. Boy. Girl. Boy.* There is no way for the plot to thicken.

I detect a fast-driving, low-riding undercurrent of glee in his face as he spills the beans, making his head shine. "It's a boy."

My sentries break into twin smiles like Cheshire cats. Time stops.

It's a boy. I, who may have the all-knowing smirk of Mona Lisa on my lips, or the gentle smile of Mary, another mother of a son, have no idea what these three words mean. The idea of a boy is as foreign to me as the idea of a baby, which is as foreign to me as the idea of being pregnant in the first place! Perhaps if he had said it's a girl, I would be smiling broadly from the heart, stimulated by self-knowledge, showered with images of little girls, two, five, seven years old, sexy, adventurous, beautiful. But no image comes. Not even the worst scenario: little boy cutting lizards in half by an old stone wall.

—*Letters to Matagalpa*

3) If you are planning to have prenatal testing, for example, an expanded AFP, a blood test to screen for the risk of neural tube or other birth defects, or an amniocentesis, a procedure to detect any chromosomal abnormalities in your fetus, you will most likely have it done between the third and fifth month of pregnancy. Prenatal diagnoses inspire a full range of confusing feelings in any pregnant woman. In the amniocentesis, for example, there is some risk involved in the procedure itself. In addition, there are all the questions that arise: What if the diagnosis detects a serious abnormality? Write down any anxiety or fear you have before the procedure. Once the test is completed, write down your experience of it. If something serious is detected, you are faced with a tremendous emotional and moral challenge—to carry the pregnancy to term or to terminate it. Write down all your feelings during this decision-making process and beyond.

After the amniocentesis, all I want is to be lifted on wings out of the subterranean and to a level where the sun can fuzz my feelings into light particles. I roll up to sitting and get off the table and onto the floor as if nothing has happened. I will have to wait two days for any complications or for their absence. Your chances are one out of two hundred. I know this but cannot feel this. . . . A nurse hands me your picture. It frightens me more than the needle had. "Why is it screaming?" I ask. The doctor tells me your mouth is open for breathing. Breathing while surrounded by fluid? I wonder. Is a fetus a fish? . . . You look like a monster, Ray Bradbury's most extreme fantasy of the diabolical infant who comprehends at least six dimensions and murders adults. . . . Later, at home, I stare at your photo for a long time. Not even with my *Oxford English Dictionary* magnifying glass can I see your sex. I sit in the chair, tender as a rose whose petals drop even before the earthquake hits. I feel no inclination to move. I am weak. I do not want to hemorrhage, cramp, or leak. Matagalpa, my monsterboy, I do not want Western medical providence to carry you away.

—*Letters to Matagalpa*

4) Close your eyes and again lay your hands on your belly. Remember the first time you really felt your baby moving? No doubt you experienced a catapult of emotions not unlike the first time you heard you were pregnant. Allow images to rise inside you. Now write a letter to your fetus-child, telling him how you felt when you first heard his heartbeat or first felt her move. Talk to this "stranger" about the relationship you feel you have with him right now.

5) You are starting a habit of more frequent communication. You now know that your fetus is not just responding to fluctuations in your body chemistry. He is actually listening. His own ears are picking up sound waves. It is your turn to listen. Does she have any questions? Is there something he wants to say? What about you? Do you have questions? Ask them and listen for his answers. Allow a dialogue to emerge in the silence of your unique communion with your child. Write it down. You are simply recording what cannot be easily known by the logical, literal mind. You must be open-minded and patient. Just as you may have heard the voice of God in prayer, or any voice whose origin you could not locate. If no words come, give yourself the gift of this silent communion.

2. "Now That It's Real, How Will I Take Care of It?"

Being pregnant is one thing, having a baby is another. If getting pregnant was like opening Pandora's box, then feeling your "inner" child move and seeing him on "TV" transforms Pandora's box into a Russian doll. Every time you open one little person, there is another one inside it! Now the worries you may have had about how your life will change when the baby comes seem to go beyond conjecture. They are becoming premonitions. How is the birth of this child going to affect your relationship with your partner? With your friends? How are you really going to be able to continue your career? When should you go back to work and how will your maternity leave affect your status? What if you don't want to go back to work after all? What if your sense of purpose and motivation is permanently altered by this pregnancy?

You may be tackled by a swarm of what-ifs as you realize you actually have to take care of the squirming infant departing from the convenience of your womb and remember that no one has trained you for this. What if, when your baby comes out, you become paranoid and hold her like a dozen raw eggs in a glass bowl or feel awkward and embarrassed and end up holding her the way a running back holds a football? What if no milk comes? What if she has colic and you start throwing your best china on the floor after six hours of nonstop crying? What if you can't tell the difference between a cry for diaper change and an opinion about the weather before anyone has invented the electronic simultaneous translator of baby whines? How is she going to fit in your house and what should you buy?

This is a perfect opportunity to chew your nails down to the cuticle. Feel free to fret to your heart's content. Rant and rave, kvetch, whine like a baby. No one is going to tell you to shut up. You can let your words pace back and forth and back and forth until they wear grooves into the floor. You have communed beautifully in perfect peace with your "inner" child. But a real baby is messier than that. How will it feel to have dark sticky excrement on your breast? To have little jaws crunching down on your blossoming aureola? To get stuck with a diaper pin? What will you do when your baby falls off the couch?

Journeying

1) Close your eyes and imagine how it would feel to hold your baby in your arms, one hand around its small buttocks, the other feeling the curve of its warm head. Imagine the smell of its breath, the feel of his tiny hand gripping your finger, the softness of her skin against yours, the feel of him sucking on your nipple for sustenance. Write down everything that comes to you.

2) Worry, whine, complain in advance. Write a list of postbirth what-ifs. What if I put the diaper on upside down? What if my partner leaves me? What if I hate my baby? What if I love my baby more than my partner? What if I don't recognize myself? Little worries, big worries, in between.

3) Shopping. What better topic is there for a North American woman in the consumer capital of the world? It has been said that a woman's shopping is a reflection of her emotional state. A pregnant woman reveals her feelings about coming to term in her attitude toward maternity clothes and baby supplies. What are your feelings? Write some anecdotes about your first adventures as a pregnant consumer shopping for the invisible customer inside you.

"She's teething. She's *teething,* I tell ya!" She was shouting into the phone. "Give her a little liquid Tylenol. Put her right to sleep." She was sitting behind an L-shaped counter in the middle of the store surrounded by so many cribs and strollers, and trainers and wind-up swings, and changers, and little clothes, and baskets of booties and diaper bags and tiny primary-color wooden benches that it looked like a festive parade for the Virgin in a small Italian town. Except this time, it was for the infant, not the Mother. "Listen, she's four months, right? She's teething!" She seemed exasperated with the ignorance of the caller, sweating like a dog in the voluptuousness of her own wisdom. . . . I, meanwhile, was walking aimlessly among baby carriages and backpacks as if I were in an ancient museum, dazzled by but distinctly remote from these relics from another time.

—*Letters to Matagalpa*

3. Surrender

Swollen like a melon in July,
lumbersome as a moose,
I've boarded that train
and I can't get off,
no return trip.

Some babies are sweet
and pink as peaches;
others are wrinkled
and scream like herons;
dispositions not optional,
all sales final.

Yet I know
that first cry
will bond me like glue,
and those wandering, wondering
dark eyes will fix my heart
faster than any lover.

—BARBARA CROOKER, "Freight Train"

There is a relentless inevitability about the course you're on. Now as you approach your third trimester, you may start to feel short of breath. Your facial skin may be darkening or changing in some way. Stretch marks may be appearing on your belly and your back may be aching with the new weight. There's nothing you can do about any of it. You couldn't hide your pregnancy from anyone even if you wanted to. You are held in the grasp of a force much bigger than you—the force that will completely transform you when you are actually giving birth. You are out of control.

The physical changes you go through during pregnancy are all a preamble for the birth itself. You have been transforming slowly but surely since the beginning. But now, were you to lie down and raise your head up, you could not see your feet even if you wore a size twelve shoe and your toenails were painted red! The size of your belly and the unpredictable movement inside it are awe-inspiring as well as alarming. Your fears are coming more into focus and becoming more specific. There is one fear that seems to supersede all the others as you take the curve into your last lap. Labor and birth. You've communed with your fetus inside you—Act I. You've had premonitions of life with your outer child pulling on your skirt—Act III. But what about Act II, whose theme is getting the bugger out of your body? It is this awesome and apparently impossible act that leads pregnant women to imagine the worst. How can a baby that big get out of a hole that small?

Fears about birth escalate. Memories of the most horrific birth stories come immediately to mind and take over the heart space. Melanie in *Gone with the Wind* and the death rate of mothers from another era, the stories of women giving birth in the 1950s, victims of sexism and the guinea pigs of experimental technologies. Memories of the woman next door with her forty-five-hour labor and the cashier at the market who gave birth in the back of a pickup truck. It seems inconsequential that the majority of women have magnificent birth stories to tell. Those are forgotten.

These fears are both typical and natural. You may feel frightened of the pain you will experience during childbirth, scared that you or your baby will be injured, or that one or both of you will die. You may feel fear of doing something embarrassing during labor or simply dread losing control of your body. You may feel scared about being on drugs and not being fully conscious during labor and birth, afraid that you will require a cesarean, anxious that your baby might be born prematurely. What if your baby is not perfect?

What if she is malformed, or even stillborn? I repeat. Such incidences are the exception rather than the rule. Yet psychologically and emotionally we must be prepared for any eventuality.

Our subconscious knows this. Birth dreams are common and frequently uncomfortable. They are preparing you for the individuation process of birth. The fetus is often represented as a small animal or an amputated limb or a tooth that is extracted as if the baby were part of your own body. Your worst fears may visit you nightly in a variety of forms. This is good. Your dreams are your own private shamanic healers. Let them do their work unhindered.

There are also conscious actions you can take in the face of the enormity of your feelings. For example, creating a more specific birth plan can, when the time comes, help you to cope with any emergency or emotional challenge that may arise. Equally important is to build a committed network of support people to be with you during the process of birth and to assist you with housework, infant care, and any other needs, foreseen and unforeseen, that will come up when your child is no longer conveniently inside you. Joining a childbirth class with your key support person(s) will help move you toward both a clearer birth plan and an educated birth support team. Meanwhile, your writing is more crucial than ever. You need to express your fears, quietly in writing to yourself, and to your closest confidantes. There is nothing to be ashamed of. You need your highest hopes as well as your worst fears to be heard.

There is nothing left to hold on to. As you approach your final trimester before birth, the word of the month is: surrender. Be the woman who goes outside when it rains and lifts her face and arms up to the sky.

Getting Ready

Close your eyes and remember times when you have felt out of control. Go back to early childhood. I lost control of my sled on wheels when I was nine and had to make a hairpin turn not to go crashing into a busy street or to cream the neighborhood witch's perfectly trimmed bushes. Continue reeling through your life. These may have been intensely happy as well as intensely harrowing experiences. Briefly write down a couple of these experiences. Write down how you felt at the exact moment you knew you were out of control.

Journeying

1) Select your worst fear about childbirth and explore it further by writing about it—how it feels, where it comes from, where it goes. Know that as you move into your last trimester before birth, your apprehension about labor and childbirth is likely to increase. Keep writing about it. You may feel like a sailor bailing out her ship in a storm. As soon as you clear the decks of water, there is more to dip your bucket into and throw overboard. Just as one fear is written down and put into perspective, another takes its place. Remember that the storm will soon be over and the sun will come out. You cannot fail in childbirth. It is impossible to do it wrong. Childbirth is simply a complex of circumstances dancing together with a particular result. Once you have taken your steps to prepare for it, your job will be simple: surrender to it. It wasn't until half an hour before my son was born that I started yelling *"Yes"* with each contraction instead of *"No, no"* into my sister's encouraging and patient face. That was the moment of surrender for me.

2) As you remember your dreams more vividly and more frequently, write them down. Dreams of being out of control, labor and birth dreams, dreams of surrender.

> I dreamed I gave birth to a baby. It was very small. I left it on the couch and went to someone else's house. While at this other house it crossed my mind that my baby's mouth might get real dry and I had a strong feeling that he was suffering, perhaps dying without access to my skin or breasts or presence on the couch. I still didn't go back right away but when I did I was feeling desperate. He wasn't on the

couch. I ran to the lighted kitchen. Two women were there who seemed like family but no one I remember recognizing. I was desperate and crying about my baby. They told me that it had dehydrated and that they had thrown it away. I woke feeling horrible, empty, devastated by the loss.

—*Matagalpa Dream Book*

3) If you or your baby has a health problem in your late pregnancy that puts either of you at risk, be sure to write down all your feelings as you surrender to whatever is best. If your care provider has put you on bed rest, write about the frustration, the tears, the inconvenience. Then thank her for giving you more time to write.

Looking at the Map

Over these past three months you have been renaming yourself mother. First, you tried on this new identity like a silky dress and walked around in it to see how it feels. Then, just when you thought you had a decent mental understanding of what it means to be a mother, you started to become one. You felt your baby move and were suddenly catapulted into that very mother-world you had just been imagining.

As you continue to write in your journal, answering the questions it asks you, your sense of yourself as a mother will become more and more palpable.

We expose weaknesses so that we can strengthen something before it falls apart, like the foundation or the hidden infrastructure of a house. You may have found weaknesses in the way you were mothered and in the way motherhood is viewed in the society. Yet you strengthened the weak spots with your own vision, conviction, and commitment to change. In this last journeying section, you revealed your fears and began to discover the power of surrendering to something larger than yourself. Redefined, self-exposed, and reinventing yourself week by week, you stand poised for the empowering third trimester, the last three months of your pregnancy.

Letter to Your Child

Write a letter to your child.

> *Querido* Orlando,
>
> *Que significa tener un niño, yo como mujer?*
>
> I am a woman. What do I know about a man? I was a girl and I remember many things about my childhood, millions of moments that a girl growing up in front of me would remind me of so that I could say, "Yes, yes, honey, I know what you mean." But what do I know about a boy? I have never been one.
>
> If I let all the men and boys I have ever known in my life amass in front of me, filling the auditorium of my memory to the rafters—my father; my grandfather; cousins; teachers; fathers of friends; my brother; his friends; elementary school crushes; classmates; boyfriends; lovers; dates; one night stands; buddies; rapists; colleagues; employers; managers; acquaintances met on a train, bus, airplane; butchers; bicycle mechanics; owners of corner stores; celluloid men I've known on the screen—all the men gathered together in suits, in overalls, in jockey shorts, the ones in front so clear you can see the wrinkles around their eyes, all packed together, getting smaller and smaller in the distance, yet with all these men that I have observed and all the boys and men that I have known, do I know anything about any of them?
>
> I know very little, Orlando. And yet you are one of them. I alone, not men, will be with you morning to night. It is I, a woman, who am carrying you in my womb, who will give birth to you, who will feed you from my own breast, who will be your caretaker, your teacher, your mother, your friend.
>
> —*Letters to Matagalpa*

Weeks 14–27

Empowering Ourselves

Your Third Trimester

Weeks 28—40

"I am myself becoming a mother."

The two identities have met like two strangers at a party. They touch. One says, "I am not myself." The other replies, "I am not yet real." They hold each other delicately, both fragile in their state of metamorphosis. The purpose of the third trimester is to affirm and celebrate this emerging identity, to experience the power of transformation in process, and to find words to express the burgeoning self, uncontainable and brilliant, like the spiritual light of a diamond.

The third trimester is a time of waiting, a magical combination of anxious anticipation, boundless energy, and unearthly calm. We walk more slowly, sit more slowly, lie down more slowly. We slow down at work or stop completely, absent-minded, in limbo between the two worlds. Birth feels imminent—exciting and powerful on the one hand, terrifying on the other. We are 99 percent body, our shifting center of gravity pulling us toward the earth. We are ripe with creation—fecund, generative, expansive, connected to the earth and to women through all time. These feelings are no longer abstract. They are visceral. We begin to feel Braxton-Hicks contractions. Relaxin is softening our pelvic joints and opening us up. Colostrum may be seeping from our nipples. Our baby is moving like molten lava inside us. It is difficult to figure out how to sleep. We find ourselves both reverent and revered.

In the following three chapters, "Letting in Love," "Celebration of

Ourselves," and "On the Cusp," we slow down to feel what it is we are becoming. Writing is like slow-motion photography. We watch our inner and outer worlds slow down dramatically so that we can see them unfold and exult in their tiniest permutations. We clothe ourselves in our wisdom and divest ourselves of vestiges of fear to notice the abundance of love around us.

With each passing day, the experience of being in limbo between the worlds may become more intense. Limbo is like nothing else. Have you noticed how free your mind is to roam in an airplane, neither here nor there, bound to no place you've ever known? During the next three months, we become shamans creating rituals. We become fortune-tellers looking into our crystal balls. Our waiting is like the wind coming down off the mountain. It knows only one way to announce its arrival: the trees dance.

We are becoming.

Seven

Letting in Love

Your Seventh Month

There is a time and a place for everything. But there is always time for love. Most women, even those of us who experienced a high degree of ambivalence about our pregnancy when we first set out upon our journey into motherhood, come to find, by the third trimester, that our feet fit the footprints in the sand. We are in love. Seagulls lift up off the pier and with them our hearts soar. As we continue our journey, we are hyperaware that we hold like a vessel the indomitable spirits of two human beings. We feel in tune with what is immeasurable. Like goddesses in training, we step out onto the beach, feeling we belong exactly where we are. Pregnancy has finally become familiar terrain. We are ready to claim our personal power without apologies. Now, in the seventh month, we have come into our own.

If your baby were to be born right now, she could survive in an intensive care nursery environment. There is nowhere to go but forward. On this journey, you have gone all the way back to the beginning—to the beginning of you. You have shown great courage simply by facing who you are, where you came from, what you are afraid of, and what you want. As you move into this final period of waiting, you take time to retrace your steps, tracking yourself through your own precious words. How have you changed? How far have you come?

In this chapter, you will have a chance to record the knowledge you have acquired and to let go of the negative emotional charge attached to certain memories so that they no longer burden you. You will use your understanding of your own life to construct a constellation of wisdom. This is how you learn to let the love in. By letting go, you free yourself to love and be loved in a multitude of ways and from all directions. Yourself, your child, your friends, your family, your God . . .

And your partner. Many of us have a traveling companion. Have you forgotten your beloved, the missing man on the map? You have been very self-involved and preoccupied with your relationship with your child. Yet once you feel your baby inside you, the lightbulb goes on. It is real, it is mine, it is *his.* What is the expectant father going through, he who is very much on a journey into fatherhood? Is he giving you the love you need in the way that you need it? And are you letting it in?

Throughout your journal writing you have grown to love yourself slowly but surely. You have taken the time to focus on the generations from which you came and the generation you are making possible. In the section called "Freeing the Birds," you will assert your power and let go of your past, your fears, and your expectations. In the section titled "Locating Ourselves: $2 + 1 = 3$," you will pay attention to your partner, your peer relationships, your own generation. Other than yourself, your child may be the most important beneficiary of your powerful pen, but he is not the only one. Through this work, you will discover that your love radius increases exponentially. Even with this new human being coming onto the stage of your life, there will be more than enough to go around!

1. Freeing the Birds

As you retrace your footprints through the roads on which you have come, you will reencounter all the birds you've caught in cages with your words. Fears, painful memories, frustrations, secrets. It is not easy to capture a bird, but you have done it repeatedly so that you could feel their beaks with your fingers and rub their feathers against your face. You have listened carefully to their incessant song and even the rhythms vibrating from their silence. Now you can simply let them go, sparrow and cockatoo, parrot and pigeon, a ritual of the imagination, symbolizing your surrender, your readiness, a gift you give yourself for the miles you have come.

Writing is healing in and of itself. You have already laid down your burdens. This section enjoins you to bear witness to and ritualize the completion of the work you have already done as you center yourself, in this last trimester, completely in the present, ready to give birth to your child. This is not to say you won't feel apprehension in the next few months, or feel unnerved by frustration or anxiety as the awesome date draws nearer, but that you have laid a strong foundation for your new and still unfamiliar identity as a mother. When you next hear the birds of fear and expectation pecking at your window, you will know how to breathe, how to write, how to escort them back into their sky. Even now, as your body's center of gravity shifts and pulls you ever closer to the earth and even though you have never weighed so much in your entire life, you feel it rising unmistakably inside you: the adorable lightness of being.

Journeying

Read with open eyes the book your life is writing and learn.

—DAG HAMMARSKJOLD

1) You have explored your relationship with your mother, your father, your past, your roots, yourself. Take this time to read what you have written and to let it into you. Your words are abundant and alive. Where they have taken you on this journey has sometimes been dramatic, sometimes subtle, always intense. You are ready now to take in all of it. You have prepared yourself for this task. After you have read your words from the beginning, sit with them for a while. Lie down. Get comfortable. Prop your belly up with pillows. Close your eyes. Do nothing. Honor your life silently without thought. Then take twenty minutes to write the essence of what you have learned on your journey thus far. Trust the ideas and the words that come to you.

2) I knew, when my son had still not arrived three weeks after his due date, that I still carried resistance to giving birth. Together with my friends, my birth partner, and my sister, I created a spontaneous ritual with owl feathers,

chanting, burning candles, the whole nine yards. We located the root of the resistance between myself and my sister and between myself and my birth partner, the two women who were to assist me through labor and birth. My younger sister and I went back to when she was born. I discovered I hated her for being born when I was two because I believed she was stealing my share of love. She remembered being hated just for existing and innocently wanting only to love me. We traded roles. I became her and spoke to her about how I felt. She became me and did the same. We cried, held each other, and finally let go, allowing forgiveness and the power of our sisterhood to reach its full potential. I went into labor that night. I was finally able to be completely vulnerable with her, and she, without reservation, was my greatest source of strength. I had let go of the part of me that still believed that bringing a baby into the world meant that I would be robbed of love. I learned that birth expanded love rather than taking it away, thereby clearing the way for my baby to be born.

Ritual is a powerful resource. We are able to let go of the things we have been attached to out of wisdom: a winning combination of perspective and choice. Perspective gives us a sense of humor. Choice allows us to let go of one idea or emotion and replace it with another. Easy come, easy go. One at a time. Like contractions during birth. Notice how wise you are. Ritualize your letting go by writing down whatever may still be blocking the birth: your most disturbing life memories, the ones that may have scarred you the deepest; your worst fears about becoming a mother, fear of giving birth to an abnormal baby, fear of your partner's infidelity, fear of death; tension or friction you may feel with someone in your birth team. Hold nothing back. Write one sentence each on a strip of paper. You can cut an 8½ x 11" piece of paper into strips and write a sentence on each one. Do this lovingly, keeping your sense of humor intact. When you are complete, burn them or put them in the recycling bin, or just sit with each one and breathe. With each breath, experience yourself letting go. When you let go of something, you will smile uncontrollably. You can't help it. You are suddenly and acutely aware of the paradox that sits at the root of human experience. Inside the fullness of attachment is the emptiness of letting go. Notice how light you feel.

Looking at the Map

A shaman is most powerful where she has been most wounded. Your writing journey through motherhood has taught you to be your own healer. Writing, learning from what you have written, and letting go: these will be your most valuable tools throughout motherhood. Old wounds will come up for you as you parent your child and remember your childhood. You will feel many emotions, some of them angry or scary, toward your child. You may not know what to do in the moment, but you will always have these tools to guide and assist you. Your child, too, will be hurt from time to time. You will be able to teach her the importance of slowing down to really feel a feeling rather than to ignore or gloss over it and with practice you will be able to model for him the miraculous power of letting go.

2. *L*ocating *O*urselves: 2+1=3

we're connecting

    foot under my rib.

I'm sore with life!

At night,

    your toes grow. Inches of the new!

The lion prowls the sky

and shakes his tail for you.

Pieces of moon

    fly by my kitchen window.

And your father comes

riding the lion's back

in the dark,

to hold me,

you,

in the perfect circle of him.

—KATHLEEN FRASER, "Poems for the New"

Forward looking and with the light at the end of the tunnel gaining in brightness, it is a good time for you to focus on your partner and to rediscover who he is in relationship to your journey into motherhood. Whether you are married to your partner or not, whether you are a single woman supported by a co-parent of your choice or in a same-sex relationship with a woman, your "partner" through pregnancy, childbirth, and raising your child is going on his or her own journey as well. That journey may be as unconscious as yours would have been if you hadn't chosen to do the writing work you have been doing. You can inspire and guide your partner. You can ask for exactly what you need and, where necessary, prepare your partner to be able to give it to you.

Like you, your partner has been full of questions from the moment he found out you were pregnant. He knows intuitively that your role as mother will compete with your role as wife. He wonders how bringing a baby into the picture will change the relationship he has with you. He may already be mourning the loss of the intimate, free-flowing life you have had together in your first childless months or years. He is asking himself if this is the best time to be a father, if he will be a good father, and what it really means to be a good father. He's remembering his own father in vivid emotional detail just as you have been remembering your mother. He is surprised and curious about the way your body is changing. He wonders, as you hurtle through your journey, crashing in and out of different identities, if he will ultimately lose the woman he used to love. Or will he love her even more than before? Flashes of the next twenty years are reeling through his mind at top speed and his dream world swells with the symbols of his own private doubts and fears.

Pregnancy gives both of you time to prepare to become a family. Taking advantage of these nine months to care for and nourish your relationship will make a world of difference in your life as parents. After all, the future happiness of a new little person is at stake. Pregnancy is guaranteed to intensify whatever emotions you already feel between you, enhancing intimacy and revealing problems that already exist. Reaffirm the closeness with words, touch, surprise gifts. Talk about the problems directly. Do not pretend they don't exist. Good, honest communication between you and your partner is essential throughout the ups and downs of pregnancy. If you are both doing cartwheels alone in different rooms, it's high time you joined forces. Talk together about how each of you is feeling. Include concerns you have about your relationship with each other and how it will be affected by the advent of three. Take care not to romanticize your cozy threesome. Your relationship as you have known it *is* in jeopardy. With a baby, it will never be the same. Sharing your journeys with each other will strengthen the bond you already have and build a foundation for the months to come.

Ellen Sue Stern, in her book *Expecting Change*, reminds us, "Your mate is the one other person in the world whose investment in your pregnancy is equal to yours; he is the single, most valuable source of support during your pregnancy."

And you must admit, as powerful and independent as you are, you could well use the support. It is not as easy as it used to be to tie your shoes, check the oil in your car, cook a five-course meal for seven, restock the photocopy machine at your office, or even to get up out of bed. Sure, you could do anything by yourself if you tried hard enough. But why lie panting on the couch after pushing up your window to let in a little breeze? Reveal your secret shameful desire to be pampered, reassured, overtly indulged. Let yourself feel dependent. You are like the sucking in of the ocean before the tidal wave . . . and that tidal wave is imminent. In three months you become CEO and janitor of your own personal twenty-four-hour child-care business (without pay). This is your last chance to be taken care of before taking care of someone else becomes your full-time occupation. No wonder you want a little pampering.

In addition to logistical assistance, you need reassurance from your partner as you've never needed it before. Deciding to have a child together represents a deepening of your commitment. However, actually having a child together can bring up many intense emotions, ranging from an almost ethereal excitement to uncomfortable or even terrifying doubts about the meaning of love, family, and the future. The divorce rate of over 50 percent leaves you wondering if you are going to be able to count on this person for the long haul. He may be wondering the same thing. Ask directly for the reassurance you need.

Let your lovemaking be your teacher during this time. Making love during pregnancy requires patience and flexibility, two critical assets for early parenting. Rehearse resolving seemingly impossible logistical challenges. Practice loving each other even as your new dual identities are emerging. Learn to express your love to the man inside the father and to the woman inside the mother. Get accustomed to the constant realization that there is, and for many years will be, someone else there "between you."

Depending on the level of stability in your relationship with your partner right now, you may find more security and trust in your female friendships at this time. Don't try to squeeze water from stone. Only other women who are familiar with your journey can satisfy certain needs you have to be understood. Spend time with the women in your life: midwives, sisters, best friends, female OB/GYNs, a particular nurse or pregnancy counselor. Share your written words with other pregnant women who are writing in their *Journey into Motherhood* journals.

Getting Ready

Take a moment to meditate on this very special person with whom you have chosen to have and raise a child. Close your eyes and remember when you first fell in love with him. See him in your mind: the way he walks, talks, expresses his emotions. What are his colors, smells, and textures? What sounds does he make? Write down images of your partner freely, openly, without reservation. Anything that comes. What qualities does he have? What does he remind you of? If you do not have a partner with you, focus on a person who will be co-parenting with you or a close friend who is giving you their support through your pregnancy and after. Keep going. Fill a whole page at random.

Journeying

1) You have learned through your writing what kind of mother you want to be. Simultaneously, you have come to understand better for yourself what it takes to be a good parent. Write down the unique qualities your partner has that will make him a terrific father. What special gifts does he bring to parenthood? When you are done, read this to him. Then make him his own personal copy. Documents that focus on the positive come in handy during difficult times. Affirmations such as this help us regain clarity when pregnancy has us bouncing off walls or early parenting seems to fragment us into a hundred multicolored pieces.

2) Write down what you need from this rare specimen of your species. Don't be shy or polite. Be direct. Include things that you may not need but that you would simply love for him do. Get his attention. Once you have written your ideas, give them to him as a gift. Talk to him about it. Find out what he feels he can give you, what you need to show him how to do, and what he absolutely can't give you so that you can find someone else to scratch that itch. Be wary of expecting your man to give you everything you need and want, yet assume that he will come through for you once he understands what you're asking for. Ask him to do the same for you. This will be a good way to get him talking about his own journey and how he's feeling. This writing will be critical to your relationship with each other once the baby is on board. Grounding yourselves in trust now, establishing the habit of honest communication before your baby is born, will lay the foundation for a strong relationship during the radically shifting fourth trimester and beyond.

3) You have reached level four of your compassion training. You started by developing compassion and forgiveness for yourself, then for your mother, then for your fetus, and now for your partner. By the time you give birth you

will be a saint by the standards of all the world's religions! Think of a major repeated argument you have had with your partner. Write for ten minutes from his perspective. Get yourself out of the way and get into his shoes. Use the first person. Be him talking to you. Do this again, thinking of a difference you have about having or raising your child. See it through his eyes. Remind yourself that your partner is your most important source of support. He is not the enemy. He simply has a different point of view rooted in his own personal and collective history. Talk to him about this history. Move steadily toward building a powerful alliance.

4) Allow a place in your journal for you to transcribe some words from your partner. Ask him to write a poem, or just a few words about how he feels as the expectant father, or his view of you as your cinematic image dissolves into motherhood. Ask him to write a letter to his child.

Cool beneath melon-colored cloth, your belly—

a joyous ripening that happens & happens,

that gently takes root & takes over,

a miracle uncelebrated under an autumn dress

that curves and falls slowly to your ankles

As you busy yourself with backyard gardening,

humming, contained, I think of your tongue

at peace in its place; another kind of fruit,

mysterious flower behind two lips that open

for air & for exits & entrances.

Perhaps if I placed

my hungry ear up next to a cantaloupe or coconut

(for hours at a time & often enough),
I'd hear a fluttering or maybe a music almost like
the story I've heard with my ear to your belly,
a sea-shell history of evolution personified. . . .

—AL YOUNG, "For Arl in Her Sixth Month"

Looking at the Map

Honest communication, compassion, acknowledgment, and appreciation are important ingredients for your relationship with everyone on your birth team as well as your partner. Ask for these and give of them generously. By doing so, you build the intimate alliances that will help carry you through the ups and downs of two months of waiting, labor and childbirth, and your first weeks—and years—of parenting. Acknowledge your entire support network. Let the love in. Then celebrate yourself in good company.

Letter to Your Child

Write a letter to your child, letting the love in.

Querido Matagalpa,
Now you are seven months. Your personality is forming, they say. You could be entering Prenatal University, learning to kick when I say kick, learning to respond to bells, learning the alphabet and a "foreign" language. What language isn't foreign to you, my silent son? You could be a university graduate in two years with the memory of megaphone waves in your ears, or clutter, or a big question mark. Is ignorance really bliss? You will already have lost the freedom of perpetual meditation. You have already heard everything: the screams of children in a police raid of a shantytown in South Africa in Dolby

stereo (I covered you with jackets in an effort to protect you), the giddy laugh of Mozart in *Amadeus* and many of his scores which you danced to, distracting me with your improvised waltzes. You have already heard everything, including an irreverent working-class artist on a poetic rampage in a small theater (you became outraged when she threw down her big floppy plastic doll, and then again and again, beating its head against the floor, you kicked angrily inside me, immediately defensive, unwilling to sit through the violence placidly and civilized like the rest of the audience). You have already heard everything, including much weeping, sirens, cars, Sweet Honey in the Rock, guttural screams of something deeper and more primal than orgasm, all kinds of music and voices at tables, in crowded streets, on the radio, TV, more people than you'd probably ever want to know, the clicking of the typewriter which might be soothing but for the long unpredictable pauses. It has not been quiet for you, has it, Matagalpa? Except by the ocean. I remember how quiet you were, how still for two whole days by the ocean where I slept in the top bunk the way I did as a child, and fell asleep listening to the waves.

—*Letters to Matagalpa*

Eight

Celebration of Ourselves

Your Eighth Month

Today she parades her shape like swellings of song,

The wings that free her, her throne, her tower.

She bursts the land with her being, her brand, her blossom,

Her passion's lofty monument, her belly's dance.

. . . Along the length and breadth of our fields the world makes its way

O everyone, run to the side. She is spacious as time.

—BOBI JONES, "Portrait of a Pregnant Woman"

Where there is love there is power. Today we can feel it. Eight weeks away from giving birth, we are full, fertile, powerful women proud of our queendom. When we move through rooms, across streets, through market aisles, into the lobby where we work, people stop what they're doing and take notice. Silently they celebrate our life-bearing power. They are moved by our courage. Inadvertently, we catalyze their spiritual development by merely passing before their eyes. We are, literally, walking miracles of first-rate proportions. How can they not transcend? That the female body can change so dramatically is beyond belief. That a woman can walk and work and talk coherently while simultaneously accomplishing the complex task of producing progeny is stunning. A young man, a stranger, escorted me across a street in my eighth month, holding back cars with his hands. Once he had guided me safely onto the sidewalk and out of harm's way, he explained his random act of kindness with this announcement: "With all due respect, you are carrying the future."

The world is watching. But we do not need the world's eyes as big as saucers to prove to us the enormity of our task. Radiant with the life-force burgeoning inside us, we already know it. We feel the promise of the future blossoming daily in our own bodies. We are ready to celebrate ourselves.

In the section called "Earth Mother," we are invited to feel the uniquely female life-force within us, to experience our connection with the earth and with all mothers through time and space, and to find a language to express our pride and sense of fulfillment as fully pregnant women. Shamelessly, we will exult in our specialness with our words.

In the section called "Locating Ourselves: Career and Motherhood," we will pay attention to how much our work is intertwined with our sense of self, how that will change and is already changing, and how we will create a life that is inclusive of our passion for work and our desire for family.

1. Earth Mother

Our bellies are eight-month fruits

fabulous with weightlessness.

We have entered summer like a state of pasture,

pregnancy like a state of mind so full

nothing else can be.

Sharing this is simple: the surprise of a tomato

still perfect after days in a pocket.

—BARBARA RAS,
"Pregnant Poets Swim Lake Tarleton,
New Hampshire"

Pregnancy is a magical point where intense spirituality and intense carnality intersect, where the miracle of creation as spirit enters the visible realm of the body. We are the weight (gravity) and the weightlessness (spirit). Our writing helps us to stop and feel this majestic and creative weaving of multiple worlds. Just as lying down on our backs where the earth herself can hold us—in a park, a field, off a mountain trail, or on a beach—reminds us how now, more than ever, we are an integral part of the universe, connected to our solar system, a citizen of our planet and a caretaker of our natural environment.

Pregnancy puts you in direct contact with the energy of creation through all of time and space. Now you are more apt to experience the earth not just as your mother, but as your sister and your friend. During labor you join forces with gravity and the entire history of life on this planet. You are earth mother. As you merge into your new identity as a mother, you learn to mother more than just your child. Recognizing the unity of all things and your membership in this unity, you learn to mother the earth, the big home of your child and your child's children. In these last few weeks of waiting and nourishment, your perspective is deeper and richer than ever. Pay attention. These moments carry prime lessons for motherhood.

Getting Ready

Set yourself down in the one place you've found that holds you and your child comfortably in its embrace. Close your eyes. Take a moment to reflect on the sacredness of the act you are committing: bringing a child into the world. Imagine mothers throughout time, each one a carbon copy of your shape. Time travel. Imagine mothers in the Stone Age, in ancient China, Mesopotamia, Aztec and Mayan mothers, mothers during the European Middle Ages, Victorian mothers, black and white South African mothers during and after apartheid, mothers in India, in Delhi, in Benares, in the dry countryside west of Bombay, North American mothers in the 1950s. Imagine pregnant women and mothers with their newborns in tow during every era of history that you are familiar with and in every country that offers you pictorial information easily. Let these women parade by in your imagination. Notice the power of the female principle that surges through you as you connect with women throughout time and space. Remember about 300,000 pregnant women around the globe will give birth on the same day as you. You are not alone. You are part of a large community, your species, your people, your family. Do you feel differently about yourself when you imagine yourself as part of something so vast and historical? Write how you feel entering this family of mothers. Describe this life-force that has entered you so completely. Write quickly and freely without thinking. Connect with the spirit that moves you.

Journeying

Empowered by your connection with the larger family of mothers and an ancient female principle rushing inside you, celebrate yourself with the song of your language. Raise your skirts so we can see the petticoats. Let your spirit shine. Start by closing your eyes and exploring the fields of your imagination. When you encounter the objects, the scenes, and the language that express you, write them down. "Know thyself" the way only metaphor can know you during this time of becoming. Art exists because nothing else does what art does. You are the artist and the creator. Inspired by these women's songs, which were modeled on Native American poet Scott Momaday's "Delight Song for Tsoai-Talee," write your own delight song. Put your name in the title: "The Delight Song of _____."

DELIGHT SONGS

I

I am the corn—knee high by the fourth of July, a forest by September
    I am the horse that first gave me wings

I am the mud of mud pies, the path that wanders and curves,

the Illinois lightning I loved to watch

I am the daughter who tells the truth

and the mother who dances the unknown

I am the question

and the exclamation point.

—Journey into Motherhood workshop participant

When you are done, go to the nearest mountaintop and proclaim your delight song to the people and countryside below. If the nearest mountaintop is your kitchen table or your front stoop, so be it. The important thing is to present yourself to the world out loud. Old shyness is water under the bridge. A sixth-grader wrote a little poem that went like this:

I want the

world to know that I

am here today.

2. Locating Ourselves: Career and Motherhood

There is no doubt about it. Becoming a mother brings into question our life mission, what it was we were put down on this planet to do. For some of us, we knew even when we were young that we were meant to have children and to contribute to the world by raising them. For others of us, we knew, at some point in our lives, that we were meant to contribute to the world through the development of a particular career. Some have experienced both of these drives together or separately at different times. The fact is, before you were pregnant, you had five, ten, or even twenty years to develop your sense of self in relation to your work. During the first trimester, "Locating Ourselves," you reaffirmed this self, this you, by connecting with your childhood, your passion, and your past. But in just eight weeks you will have a baby in tow. Now what?

There are many issues braided into the question of work. Two, I think, are the most important: money and passion, not necessarily in that order. You must survive. Therefore you have to consider loss of income, when to return to work, if you want to return to work, how to manage child care logistically and financially, and how to share the responsibility of child care and income with your partner.

Beyond survival there is passion. Passion is what allows us to thrive in our lives. I speak now of passion that drives you out of the private and into the public sphere to serve, to contribute, to invent, to lead, to satisfy the complex human need for self-development in a societal context, to nourish the intellect, or simply to socialize with peers. This passion comes in many forms and seems to expose itself in stages throughout our lives but it is always there waiting in the brush like a tiger ready to pounce.

Before you lose yourself in motherhood, you need to pay attention to it. What is your current relationship with your work/career? Perhaps you are in love with your work and feel called upon to do it. Or you may not experience a sense of mission about your work, yet it is what you do most of your waking hours and there is something about it that satisfies you, that fulfills an important need you have. Or perhaps you are floundering, not yet sure of your calling. No matter what relationship you have with your work right now, it is a given that for the next few years you will have a baby and then a toddler in tow, and even when your toddler is a little older, it is very difficult even to think when your child is around needing and demanding your attention. What will you do? How will you graft motherhood onto your growing career or graft your career back onto your growing motherhood? Millions of women with children work and are facing this same dilemma. The conflict between who you are as a childless adult in the world and who you will be as a mother goes to the heart of your sense of self. New motherhood contains within it, among other things, a full-fledged identity crisis.

I have good news. You are perfectly capable of actually thriving in your dual roles of mother and career woman. For one thing, all of your writing thus far has been preparing you for this crisis. For another thing, it is not unresolvable. Although you will experience some degree of conflict for years to come, that powerful You that you have just been celebrating can and will create a life that beautifully, if not always gracefully, encompasses both your passion for work and your desire for family.

If, on the other hand, you feel certain even now in your eighth month, or soon discover upon holding your baby to your heart, that mothering itself is the work you are meant to do (and can afford to do without holding another job), you have chosen an admirable path. Make yourself at home. Indulge in your passion for mothering and raising children. Have more than one. Start a preschool. Take advantage of the purity of your desire for as long as it lasts. And if, at some point, you feel destiny calls you in a different direction, listen to it.

Whatever you choose to do and whenever you choose to do it, your children will benefit from your following your passion rather than ignoring it.

Getting Ready

To understand any possible conflict that may arise, you first need to clarify your sense of purpose. Ask yourself these questions: What is your passion? What do you feel called upon to do in this world, no matter how seemingly big or small? What do you feel you could not live without doing? What is your soul's work? If you feel uncertain about what your mission or ultimate career choice is, attending to these questions will help bring your possibilities into intimate focus. Answering them without thought, without pressure, and without feeling attached to any particular outcome, will give you the freedom to explore them. Write down the answer that comes to you. Let the truth come into view slowly but surely without thinking or planning. Even if there is no clear answer, you will come to a better understanding of what is most meaningful to you. Child or no child, what is it you want to have accomplished, created, or experienced in this world before you die?

Journeying

1) At work you are not the same employer or employee you used to be. Particularly now, in your third trimester, you feel the physical strain of your normal workload. Filled with your rich inner world, you cannot help but daydream or become easily distracted. Co-workers may be repeatedly asking you if and when you intend to come back to work or may be insisting that you can never combine your work with your journey into motherhood, as if the two were mutually exclusive. You may feel alienated or unduly pressured. Our society isn't yet used to having very pregnant women continuing to give sales presentations, lead board meetings, or carry on just as before in the professional workplace. You may feel your need to be emotionally and physically available to your child already dominating your desire to work. Write down how you have been feeling being pregnant at work.

When you are done, write down what it is you need in order to feel respected and supported in your work. Then ask for it, including a maternity leave that suits you. Remember these affirmations suggested by Ellen Sue Stern in her book, *Expecting Change*, and then add your own.

- I have a right to keep working during my pregnancy.
- I have a right to have a baby without jeopardizing my career.
- I'm not just any employee, I'm a pregnant employee.

2) Imagine the best of all possible worlds. What is your vision of how you can combine your career with your role of mother? What would it look like?

Use the best out of what you have known, but then go beyond what your mother did, what your friends are doing, what you've assumed to be true. This is not utopia or crazy dreaming. This is empowered envisioning, the radical idea that you can actually carry out. Include how you see your partner as well as your friends, family, or co-parents fitting into your vision. I like to remind myself of the saying: it takes a whole community to raise one child. This is very important. You may often feel alone in your motherhood as if you were the only responsible caretaker of your child. In Chapter Seven, in the section called "Locating Ourselves: $2 + 1 = 3$," you established your support network, your extended family. Rely on them. Continue to ask them for what you need. Remind them that "your" children are the responsibility of all of us. Traditional marriage and the practice of division of labor by gender have not caught up with feminist theory or the fact that most women with children also work for income. Include in your vision how it would look if you were sharing child care and child rearing equally, or at least substantially, with your partner. What would it look like if you were supporting each other, in theory and *in practice*, to pursue your dreams both in your careers and in your parenting? The experience of motherhood is never the same as what we imagine it to be. You will need to revise your vision somewhat once you settle into motherhood. But your conviction now will give you strength when you are ready to take on the challenge of living in your passion in both your private and public spheres. Write down your vision.

Looking at the Map

Your own personal visionary, the one your words wake up inside you, sees how the Self with all her longings, ambitions, and passions will be able to integrate with your motherhood self once you are a mother. You have experienced the power of becoming. You have let the love in and felt your child, your partner, and your birth team to be your allies. Your journey has been long and arduous at times. Yet here you are, ready to enter your last month of pregnancy: full of child, full of love, full of life.

Letter to Your Child

Write a letter to your child, full of your passion.

Today my skinny Lamaze instructor with her giddy voice showed us the birth process using a birth atlas so big she disappeared every time she held it up for us to see so it seemed as if the uterus itself were talking. "This is the baby at eight months," it said. "Notice the mucous plug." "Here is an effaced cervix." Et cetera. I had never seen drawings of the fetus like this before. They had always been miniature scientific drawings or one-dimensional black-and-white sketches or photographs. These renderings were life-size and three-dimensional: the uterus, placenta, and fetus done in white alabaster against a rich blue background.

Some voice inside me had to admit you are as substantial as Christ in Michelangelo's "Pieta" and not, in fact, a little wet mouse, or a worm, or a small plastic doll as you have repeatedly been in my dreams. *This is what you have inside you!* I have needed someone to hammer it home to me, trap me in a small room with no distraction and put the pictorial fact in my face. All along, my stubborn prince of denial has needed this single illustration to require me to comprehend truly the weight of your round head, bigger than a ripe grapefruit, fitting into my own cervical dome, and your rump, two-cheeked like a split head of lettuce or two eggplants, smooth and perfect in the center of my body, your thighs bent down toward the back and then bent again at the knees so that the pudgy little feet each with five pink toes reach back up to the top of my womb-globe just under my bull dozing breasts, ripe for your sucking. The whole world seems to be screaming the words, *This is what you have inside you.*

I am not ready, Matagalpa. I'm not ready for you to come out of the realm of fiction, the invisible recipient of all these letters, the empty character that I made up.

—*Letters to Matagalpa*

Nine

On the Cusp

Your Ninth Month

it is a hot wind the breathing

is strong and heavy

nine months pregnant you scrub

the floor and the back porch

and the steps

there is so much energy

the beans are picked and stored

for tomorrow's supper and today

the rosebush pushed past

its old mark on the windowsill

this is the last day of summer. . . .

what is it the body knows

as it dances across the room

for no reason. . . .

tonight you go to sleep

    the alarm clock set

> *the body*
>
> *already turning its face*
>
> *toward the open road*

—HELEN HOFFMAN, "Night Journey"

Time seems to stop. Your baby can be born safely from now on. She can see and hear and even her lungs have matured for breathing the air you breathe. Physically, the focus of your body is no longer on development of the baby but on preparing both of you for the big exit. The baby drops down against the cervix, so snug now in your womb, he can barely move. This adds to the quietness of this period. He is waiting, too, and you may wonder what he is thinking as he rests upside down cradled by your pelvis with nowhere to go but out. Braxton-Hicks contractions become more frequent, more intense, and are sometimes painful so that it seems that labor has already begun. All difficult feats require practice and giving birth is no exception. The imminence of birth sits like an eagle on a promontory over your head, regal and silent, anticipation for the dive so intense in her darting eyes, you can already see the field mouse mangled in her mouth. You may feel restless and energetic or languorous and dreamy.

Around the world in every culture this is a very special time. The word of the month is *opening*. In *The Life Within*, Jean Hegland tells us, "In India and Ireland, Siberia and the Americas, and among the wandering Gypsies, the whole of an expectant mother's house and life becomes metaphor for her labor, and so doors must be opened, hair loosened, pots uncovered, animals set free, all so that there will be no obstructions or hesitations when she gives birth." The whole world seems to be watching, alerted to the imminent birth of one of their species. The human race instinctively desires continuation. You represent this for everyone else. With the best of intentions and without even thinking, they will make every effort to make sure you succeed in bringing forth their brethren. You may receive unsolicited advice. As always, your job will be to remain true to your own needs, to listen to your own voice.

There is tremendous power in the birth traditions of ancient cultures.

In their essence they make sense even to us, with our predominantly industrialized, high-tech mental constructs about childbirth. The opening, the loosening, the complex systems of what is lucky and what is unlucky for a pregnant woman to do, or say, or hear, or see when she is on the brink of giving birth create a highly directed and, ultimately positive, energy around the birth itself. We may all express it differently, but in every culture we are essentially sitting in a circle around the birthing woman chanting: May the baby come out easily, may it come swiftly, may it come auspiciously and in good health.

One of the express purposes of your writing journey thus far has been to open you up to this moment. Continue to clear the decks with your words by writing and speaking what is true for you.

Your ninth month is also a kind of closing as you approach the end of your pregnancy. Libby Colman notes, in *Pregnancy: The Psychological Experience*, that "photographers and painters have captured this [time] best when they show the pregnant woman standing serenely at a window, emphasizing the extent to which her experiential world is taking place on the inside, but with a reminder that it is on the brink of making the transition, of passing through the window into the world beyond." There is something melancholy about this time as is true of all closures. The depth and richness of your inner life as well as your ease in accessing it during pregnancy is coming to an end. It will become harder to access it after birth. You will have passed through that window you stood next to and into the bright fresh air together with your child. Keep your journal with you to remind you of that precious world behind the looking glass.

In these last weeks you will write often to your child and have a chance to say good-bye to your pregnancy.

1. Crystal Ball

Birthing brings me

to a continent's ledge

dissolved above and below

food for the moon's blistering tongue

Birthing brings   fear's tight-fisted heart

deep breathing to beat easy

When I break open,   they said

gore and ocean pour from the guts

And will the salt spray sting?

Will pelicans lift throats full of fish?

Will I laugh

when beyond the water's howl

birds click and caw

twisting in the juicy cave

a throat constricts to sing

with birthing screeches

And will I sing?

—SUSAN SUNTREE, "Birthing Brings Me"

What will it be like? On the cusp of birth you want to know once and for all how everything will go for you at childbirth. What will your baby look like, what noises will she make, what will he do? What will it feel like to hold your infant in your arms?

You have voyaged deep into the jungle of pregnancy, perhaps forgetting that you had once been somewhere else or that there was ever going to be another country filled with adventures ahead of you. You are like a hiker making her way from Colombia to Argentina through the Brazilian rain forest. Before you know it your days are filled with the reality of toucans, dripping foliage, and tropical sun. Your past and future seem to disappear in the presence of such abundant life. But you will come out of your pregnancy just as the hiker will leave the perfumed rain forest and reach her destination. Your stomach will be flat again. And even your baby, which has seemed throughout your pregnancy to be your final destination, will not, in fact, be cooing and sucking your breasts for decades to come. Miraculously, there is life beyond "baby": a little boy or girl learning to read, a foulmouthed teenager borrowing your car, a mature man or woman getting promoted at work, grandchildren lent to you over summer vacation.

The section called "Crystal Ball" lets your imagination take you into this future. Your words will open the window and then build the imaginary road for your newborn to crawl out on, the universe of galaxies winking at his upturned face.

Getting Ready

Let the absence of words open your heart up to a new beginning. Get out your crayons or colored pens and *look into your crystal ball.* Imagine your cervix and birth canal opening for birth. Draw the opening like a flower, like an ocean, or in whatever form it comes to you. Now draw your baby coming through the opening. Grease the joints of reality with your pens. If the hormone relaxin doesn't do it, your drawings will release you, offering up your bounty, drawing forth your child like drawing water from a well.

Journeying

1) Imagine you are a golfer. You've been out on the greens aiming your strokes toward some invisible pocket "over yonder" for eight long months. But now you can see the hole in front of you, the one that fits the ball exactly. The hole is your labor and birth. Your feelings of anxiety and excited anticipation feel visceral. Imagine your childbirth now, from this more intimate perspective.

Look back at exercise 1 in the "Childbirth" section of Chapter Two when you first visualized yourself giving birth. At that point, early in your pregnancy, you knew little about childbirth and had not yet developed a strong communication with your fetus. Being pregnant didn't seem quite real. Now you are a different woman. Everything is real. You have an intimate relationship with your unborn child. You are wiser, deeper, able to let go. Use your first innocent inclinations from that earlier exercise as a foundation for the imaging work you are doing now. You are on the cusp of being a mother and the qualities of motherhood that you yourself have defined are already demonstrating themselves in your daily life. Let your Self and your Mother inform each other as you imagine the birth of your child.

Look into your crystal ball. What are you taking with you to your hospital, or, if you're going to have a home birth, what have you assembled to have around you? You are already equipped with a birth plan that has been clearly communicated to your medical providers and your birth support team over these past weeks. Envision the gift of birth you are going to give to your child. Watch it take place before your very eyes. If you have trouble imagining how your baby will feel to you as she is coming out, think of a watermelon and imagine giving birth to that. Briefly write down what happens. Include everything: the various stages of labor, your water breaking, your cervix dilating, pushing, giving birth to your baby, releasing your placenta, cutting the umbilical cord, your first contact with your newborn. Now look again. Imagine a different scenario. Write this one down, and a third one if you want to. Then sit silently for a moment with your journal. Notice the admirable preparation you have done and remind yourself that life is ultimately beyond your control. Experience this paradox and decide to accept the birth the world gives you. The birth I actually had was radically different from any of the many scenarios I had ever imagined. Still, there was great beauty in it.

2) It is time to expect a real baby and not a fantasy.

> If your visions of motherhood consist of nothing but leisurely morning walks through the park, sunny days at the zoo, and hours coordinating a wardrobe of miniature, sparkling clean clothes, you're in for a heavy dose of reality shock. There'll be many mornings that

will turn into evenings before you and your baby ever have the time to see the light of day, many sunny days that will be spent largely in the laundry room, and few tiny outfits that will escape unstained by spit-up pureed bananas and baby vitamins. And if you have images of bringing a cooing, enchanting Gerber baby home from the hospital, you are headed for certain postpartum disillusionment. Not only won't your newborn be smiling or cooing for many weeks, he or she may hardly communicate with you at all, except to cry—most notably when you're sitting down to dinner or starting to make love, have to go to the bathroom, or are so tired you can't move.

—ARLENE EISENBERG, HEIDI EISENBERG MURKOFF, SANDEE EISENBERG
HATHAWAY, *What to Expect When You're Expecting*

Look into your crystal ball. Write down what you imagine your actual experience of your baby will be like. Write down the images you find most gratifying as they march through your mind. Write down the images that are most disturbing. The yin and the yang. The dark and the light. Write with a sense of humor knowing there is nothing like the real thing.

3) *Look into your crystal ball.* Visualize yourself with your child when she or he is one year old. Notice your surroundings, the colors and texture of what is around you. What are both of you wearing? What noises is your child making? What are you both doing? Then imagine yourself and your child at six years old, perhaps the first day of school or tucking her into bed. What does her face look like? What is she saying? Notice the smells, the sounds, the colors, the light, all the details of the moment. What are you both doing? How do you feel? Keep going. See yourself with your child at ten, at twenty, at thirty. Let the images come up for you along with the feelings. Write these down.

> *in the next room my children sleep*
> *I hear them grow in the dark,*
> *hearts ticking like clocks;*

teeth erupting like volcanos;

teeth loosening like ripe fruit—

cell by cell,

the muscles stretch   the bones lengthen,

a silent internal construction,

a reservoir of growth—

dreams bursting like dams

they grow in the night—

loaves of bread slowly rising with sweet-smelling yeast;

and just the sound of their breaths in the dark—

is a feast.

—PHYLLIS CAPELLO, "listen . . ."

2. Ship at Sea

And so we wait, poised between our two worlds,

until the waiting seems stable, fixed

as though we would remain forever

in these hugely pregnant days.

—JEAN HEGLAND, *The Life Within*

Now, in your last month, you are like a ship at sea, an ocean liner among the sailboats of other women, rocking steadily and sometimes tossed by the waves beneath you. Far out at sea, you silently rock surrounded by the vastness of the ocean, no land in sight. You are full of your passenger and waiting. Not used to celestial navigation, you look up at the sky, looking for the constellation that will tell you when your child is coming, when and where land will be sighted, when you will be able to walk barefoot onto the shore with a baby in your arms. You wonder, when the falling star streaks across your view, if it means that the sky is spilling its secrets for you to decode. You look for meaning in ordinary events, search everywhere for a sign from on high.

We in the Western world have been born for four generations into a scientific world where things can be measured, where prognoses can be made, where people are goal oriented and want results. If there is a due date, they want to hear the squeal of the babe like the cock's crow at dawn on that day. They do not want to accept that there is mystery in something so mundane. It scares them to death to imagine high-tech medicine does not know why labor starts when it does, that they cannot predict exactly when it will happen. And so we all set our hopes on the due date because science and medicine give us the secure illusion that there is one. Yet if you are "late," you are in good company. Many women, especially those giving birth for the first time, give birth later than their due date. Your child will come when he is ready and not before.

Getting Ready

You wrote about your body in the second month when your waist was still a waist. What about now? Do you realize that the shape you have right this minute has been worshiped throughout the ages? Think of yourself as a fertility goddess. Compare your ripe body and the way you are feeling in and about your body to objects in the world. What does the physical state you're in remind you of? The fertility of your imagination is at its peak. Take advantage of this to come up with wild and woolly images heretofore unheard of and never to be repeated by any woman anywhere any time. Experiment with your language. Invent words. Surprise even yourself.

Journeying

1) The list of possible physical symptoms for this period sounds like a geriatric's diary: hemorrhoids, heartburn, leg cramps, backaches, swollen ankles, leaking liquids, constipation, and varicose veins. Not to mention insomnia, the discomfort of carrying around the equivalent of two laptop computers around your waist, and the thrashing and squirming of a live object that somehow got trapped inside you. You are "99 percent body." Have you tried posing on the beach in a sexy bathing suit? Write about what it is like to live your life inside this body. What complex strategies does it take to accomplish simple tasks? What hardships do you face on a daily basis that would have seemed preposterous just a few months ago? And what about your superhuman vitality? You may be experiencing bouts of energy so robust, it would take three muscular people to keep you from reroofing your house by yourself. Record the tragicomic moments of the denouement of your pregnancy. Discover threads of hilarity in your immeasurable discomfort. And listen to the wisdom of your intelligent body. "What is it the body knows as it dances across the room for no reason?"

> I feel like a cannonball with the weight of you. Especially in bed. On my back, even with pillows behind my head, you sink down below the mattress pulling me with you as a steel fishing weight pulls the bait to the floor of the deep blue sea. . . . And I wonder, because my womb is hot and heavy, rehearsing for labor with five, ten, fifteen Braxton-Hicks contractions a day, when will someone ignite the gunpowder at the back of the cannon and send you flying out of my birth canal, up into the sky and back into my arms?
>
> —*Letters to Matagalpa*

2) In your last few weeks, you experience Braxton-Hicks contractions and other physical signs that labor is imminent. And yet your child does not come. You are in limbo between the two worlds. Write about this strange and

spiritual time of waiting. How are you feeling? What are you imagining? What does this period remind you of? Are you searching for signs from the universe, a full moon, an empty toothpaste tube? What are people saying to you? What is your baby saying to you? What are you saying to yourself? If you become "overdue," the sensation of being in limbo can magnify to outrageous proportions. Continue to write your feelings down.

The world is watching, Matagalpa. They're telling me: "Have orgasms!" "Masturbate!" "See an X-rated movie in the front row." Anything, they say, that will translate my body into a pulsar emitting light waves in or out of bed. "Take castor oil." "Drink rock tea." "Try blue cohosh." "Walk up hills." They are all waiting. As though you were coming for them somehow. "Maybe needles in your kidney points will help." "Eat spicy foods." "Sit next to your stereo speakers turned up to their highest volume." Each one has their own labor theory: how to start the engine of a dead car. They lay their hands on me. They call me repeatedly on the phone. "So where is he?" "When is he coming?" They have things to do. "Friday would be good for me," says one. "No, not Monday!" says another. "I can't wait much longer," says a third. For me it is not a matter of convenience. It is my whole life.

—*Letters to Matagalpa*

3) There is a ceremony you can do for your child that will be an invaluable gift to both of you. Include your partner in this ritual. Ask yourselves what is your greatest wish for your child. What do you dream for her? Be spontaneous. You will find much beauty in whatever words come to your lips, no matter how simple. Write down your answers. At your shower, have each person come put their hands softly on the roundness of your belly, and tell you their wish for your child. Record it with a tape recorder or with a friend who is comfortable doubling as a speedy scribe. Later write these down in your journal and add them to your own.

4) Take a quiet moment to notice how you feel ending your pregnancy. Personally, I wanted it to go on for another year! Allow yourself space to mourn the end of this extraordinary part of your journey into motherhood and with it the end of your life as you have known it. Go with your partner or a close friend on one last two-day vacation, or simply take a long walk or have a long romantic dinner. Write down how you feel being on the cusp, laying one rich chapter of your life to rest and starting a new one.

Looking at the Map

Everything you have learned during your pregnancy has prepared you for childbirth and will serve you throughout your life as a mother. The risk factors for labor and childbirth listed in the Eisenbergs' *What to Expect When You're Expecting* are also the essential instructions for your entire journey into motherhood. Reflect on each one for a moment. Notice the parallels between the awesome task of giving birth and life itself. Let this be your childbirth meditation. 1) Take one contraction at a time. 2) Nourish yourself and know you deserve it. 3) Know enough about yourself and your process to feel some measure of control and confidence. 4) Don't experience pain in advance (expecting it) but surrender to the moment. 5) See the good in the bad—in childbirth this means: concentrate on what the pain is accomplishing; in life, it means: learn from tragedy, then use and teach what you have learned.

There is no room for pity. In childbirth as in life, you can choose not to succumb to feelings of helplessness because you have learned ways to help yourself. You can remember that you are not alone, because you have let in love, and learned how to ask for what you need. Slowly but surely you have been building your throne.

Now you stand on the threshold of an extraordinary world. The birth force is on your doorstep. Trust her. Like you, she is reliable in her mission.

Letter to Your Child

These are your last opportunities to talk to your "inner" child before you hold her against your breasts. From the depths of the wisdom that has grown in you throughout your pregnancy, what insights or advice do you have to share with her? What feelings? What last words do you have to give to your fetus before birth?

Reminder: In this last month, write to your child often, even every day.

Like this moon after a whole day of pouring rain, you are, Matagalpa, within range of your own entry into this clean night. No longer as distant as the stars. Still there will be a meteor as you pass from relative purity to relative impurity, flaring up with your tail lit splendidly as you pass through the stratosphere between my legs. The moon falling from the sky to earth between my thighs, the whole circle of the head entering into the visible sky, just a slice crowning white in the bright light of the hospital room where everything is discreet, no longer the unity of the womb—but rather the four white walls, the two chairs, the doorframes, the built-in blood-pressure machine, the square tiles on the floor, the boundaries of the bed. Even though your eyes are locked shut, you squint behind the brightness. Your lids cannot protect you. You are the moon reflecting the bright fire of the sun on your body. You cannot escape the brightness, the discreteness, the tangible quality of things.

—*Letters to Matagalpa*

Weeks 28–40

Being Ourselves

Your Fourth Trimester

Weeks 1–12

"I am myself and I am a mother."

We have crossed the line, leaving the threshold into motherhood behind. And yet our journey is not over. The identity journey speeds up after birth, having been given a jolt by the physical presence of an infant in the house. In the first few weeks, the self is likely to feel swallowed up by the new mother identity that is no longer an abstraction. Even if a pregnant woman feels that she has completely accepted the idea of being a mother, the pure taste of motherhood can be overwhelming. The integration of her old and new identities is still very much in process and it is a strange process indeed. It is not as if a woman suddenly one day recognizes her deflated but inflatable self in her new mother identity: "Oh, hello! I remember you. Now, what was your name?" Selves are not so finite or distinct. It is more like sighting familiar flags on a piece of foreign land and saying with a sigh, "I belong here, too." It may happen right away or it may take months or even years for the woman to feel rooted in the wisdom of true integration in which there is no dissonance. Yet slowly the self finds itself within and together with the new identity. What had felt like dual worlds and dual selves comes together in a sacred union—a synthesis for which no one has invented a name.

The purpose of the fourth trimester is to complete this process. In "Coming Out," "Down Under," and "Courage and Acceptance," we welcome the "watermelon" we've given birth to, surprisingly soft and warm in our beds; we face and fully experience both the magic and the mundane of early motherhood; we recognize and express whatever identity conflict actually exists within us; and, finally, we become whole again. The first weeks after giving birth are a private, strange, and bewildering time—"ineffable, inexplicable, unprecedented in life experience," writes Libby Colman. Motherhood and the baby, too, seem hyperreal. The new mother feels engulfed in them as her body slowly recovers from the trauma of giving birth. The rest of life (anything that doesn't bear directly on the life of the baby, including the world outside the woman's front door) seems unreal, oddly irrelevant, and foreign.

As the third month after birth rolls around, the new reality begins to settle into something real, something authentic. Our babies can hold up their heads. They know where their hands are in relation to things they can touch, and they long for someone to respond to their smiles and "talk," the makings of true love. By the end of the fourth trimester, they recognize our face among a crowd and infinitely prefer ours. Meanwhile, we have rallied to the task of mothering and, as our babies become more expressive of their individuality, we feel the very love they long for tugging at our hearts. Reality seems to conspire with our journaling to bring our two powerful evolving identities into harmony.

In the next three months there is an abundance of learning going on, a kind of mothering intensive. We are learning how to take care of our babies. We are learning how to balance the needs of ourself, our partner, and our child. We are learning who we are as mothers.

Our babies could well be our best teachers. We would be wise to watch and listen to our little ones. We may have been involved in a process of learning for decades, yet we are not so wise as this.

We are ourselves.

And we are mothers.

Ten

Coming Out

Your Tenth Month

That's the moment I always think of—when the

slick, whole body comes out of me,

when they pull it out, not pull it but steady it

as it pushes forth, not catch it, but steady it

as it pushes forth, not catch it but keep their

hands under it as it pulses out,

they are the first to touch it,

and it shines, it glistens with the thick liquid on it.

That's the moment, while it's sliding, the limbs

compressed close to the body, the arms

bent like a crab's rosy legs, the

thighs closely packed plums in heavy syrup, the

legs folded like the white wings of a chicken—

that is the center of life, that moment when the

juiced bluish sphere of the baby is

sliding between the two worlds,

wet, like sex, it is sex,

it is my life opening back and back

as you'd strip the reed from the bud, not strip it but

watch it thrust so it peels itself and the

flower is there, severely folded, and

then it begins to open and dry

but by then the moment is over,

they wipe off the grease and wrap the child in a blanket

    and

hand it to you entirely in this world.

—SHARON OLDS,
"The Moment the Two Worlds Meet"

Your baby is here! This is the number-one pivotal reality of the moment, filling your life screen as if nothing else ever existed. If you didn't have your journal, you might be speechless. This is a very internal and private time dominated by memories of your birth experience and a hyperawareness of the strangeness and vulnerability of your baby. Your body has just gone through the most dramatic change possible. You need to give yourself this time to regain balance in your body. Keep the sharks at bay. You are faced with suddenly separating from the baby inside you, accepting the reality of your child and giving up the fantasy of the child you expected. This is a time of closeness and intimacy between you and your baby, between you and your partner. At the same time, you are suddenly a woman with a baby at her breast desiring comfort and security. You are utterly exhausted, stressed with radical hormonal changes, faced with the irrevocable reality of this tiny dependent being. Your baby isn't the only one feeling vulnerable. You, too, feel extremely vulnerable in the first weeks after birth. Yet all around there's been a shift of attention from you to the baby. Many new mothers experience the "blues" the first week, some much longer. As impossible as it may seem, it is important that you take the time to write, to reflect, to get perspective.

1. Frame That Watermelon

When your guest arrives there is only one thing to do: welcome her. Welcome her with all your heart. The first encounter is the purest moment. There will be plenty of time for impurities: questions, fears, and anxieties as the different layers of your new and stunning reality come to the fore and fall into place. Now is the time to savor the innocence of pure love washing over you.

As you greet this new member of the tribe with all the exuberance you can muster, you may find yourself preoccupied with the events of his birth. You may well want to go over your birth story blow by blow with the help of others who were present. We are so intensely focused on moving our child out, on our breath, and the pain, that we often don't really know what was going on around us. We may lose our sense of time in the throes of contractions. Yet many of us find it important to reconstruct the details of this life-changing occasion, the miraculous moment when the two worlds meet. This is the beginning of a legend, the legend of your child, which you will weave together for quite some time.

In addition to being a threshold for you, the birth is a pivotal event for your child. Some feel that the birth experience—how each of us came into the world—has a significant effect on our temperament, our psyche, on our understanding of the world. My own son, exactly a year after his birth, to the minute, relived the birthing process spontaneously in my arms. I thought he was possessed with a demon. He contorted and stretched uncontrollably for about half an hour, twisting his head into impossible angles. Then, just as suddenly, he became quiet, exuding a serenity I had previously only attributed to saints. As he rested in utter peace, his eyes open and ready to be in the world, I felt intuitively that he had just exorcised the physical and emotional pain of birth from his body. And, I felt liberated along with him.

In this section you will use your words to reconstruct your childbirth experience in all its dimensions.

Getting Ready

Write a welcome song/poem to your baby. Allow the first sounds to come forth out of your speechlessness. Let them be wild. Let them be woolly. Let the sounds gurgle to the surface like the first sounds of an infant, making no sense, simply delivered! This is a love like no other love.

O my mole, sudden & perfect

golden gopher tunneling

to light, o separate(d)

strands of our breath!

 Bright silver

threads of spirit

 O quicksilver

spurt of fist, scansion of

unfocussed eyeball,

 grace of yr

cry, or song, my

cry or

 you lie warm, wet on the

soggy pelt of my

 hollowed

belly, my

Leslie Kirk Campbell

bones curve up

to embrace you.

—DIANE DI PRIMA, "The Loba Sings to Her Cub"

Journeying

Write your birth story. Talk to others who were there. Get more details until you feel complete. What happened? What happened next? A blow by blow account. Include the smells, the sounds, the textures, the light. Write down the words your partner said to you, the words your witnesses remind you that you said to them, or to your child, or to God. For most of us, our births go quite differently from anything we had imagined. Writing down what actually happened will help you sort out and understand your childbirth experience. Keep in mind that in the end, no matter how many times you go over the incidents in your mind, not everything that happened during the miracle of birth will be explicable. I will never completely understand why we never went to the hospital where I had been planning to give birth even though my contractions were coming fast and furiously. Yet the result was beyond everyone's expectations: I gave birth naturally at home in my bathtub with the serendipitous assistance, in the last ten minutes of pushing, of a friend who is a midwife, without any doctors, machines, drugs, or vaginal tearing, to a perfectly healthy nine-and-a-half-pound baby.

If your birth story has had a tragic ending, stay connected with your birth "family," your allies on this journey. Writing down all of your feelings can help you come to terms with this immeasurable loss. Know that the journaling you've done thus far will strengthen you in your mourning and in your healing.

Elsa was born under the full moon

on the first day of Spring.

Everyone in the room bore her forth.

My job was in a way the easiest

albeit the most terrifying.

I had to look the Birthforce in the eye

and get out of the way

while it drove through my body

like thunder through tissue paper

demanding that I open up. . . .

—JESSICA MURRAY, "Elsa's Birth"

2) Birth and death are our finest teachers. I believe that every child should witness a human birth as foundational to their education. Let your own child's birth provide you with the teachings inherent in it. You have spent months worrying about this single event, perhaps terrified about it. You had planned it and imagined it more than once. The answer to all this preparation is life itself. What spiritual lessons do you find? What psychological lessons are hidden in the way you responded to pain, to change, to risk, to support or lack of it, to the unforeseen twist in the way everything worked out? What did you learn about your own ability to assert your needs? About chaos and order? About fantasy and fact? About the power of your intuition? Were you prepared? And what, by the way, is the meaning of providence?

> Nothing is how it was meant to be. Or perhaps everything is precisely how it was meant to be on some other plane than the one my calendar adheres to, somewhere in the interstices of the collective unconscious, ancient and crowded with the screams and laughter of women giving birth through time on piles of straw, on dirt floors, on mats, in fields, on cots, on quilted mattresses, alone or surrounded by a few women whose faces are raw with the painful and beautiful inevitability of the moment which they too have known.
>
> —*Letters to Matagalpa*

2. The Madonna in Me

One taste of you and I stop,

caught with a lump in my throat

and a clue

That my sustenance will come

from emptying myself to you.

—DORIS FERLEGER, "Emptying"

From between the two worlds, your child has come completely into this one. You, for whom motherhood has long been an abstraction, who have been preparing for motherhood for months, now find yourself smitten by it like a new lover—but sweeter than anything you have ever experienced. You look in a mirror and you can't believe what you see, your face softened by birth and fatigue, your baby in your arms as if he had always belonged there. You suddenly recognize yourself in Michelangelo's "Piéta" and a million other sculptures and paintings of the Madonna with her child, the most popular mother in the Western world.

Especially in the first days, you unconsciously claim your motherhood. You can't help it. You are filled with it. You become Mother before you settle into mother. Savor this time and the innocence and purity of these feelings. Feel the tenderness of your love, the total dependency of your infant, the immense responsibility you suddenly have to take care of a human life.

Most of you will experience an immediate bonding between you and your newborn, a love like no other love, an intensity of feeling like you have never felt. Think about it for a moment. There is no one else in our lives with whom we are so intimate, so physically close for so long. In the belly, united in a symbiotic relationship, and then outside, the invisible emotional umbilical cord remains strong.

Bonding is an expression of empathy and connectedness that has been growing in you throughout your pregnancy. Your bond is no longer to a fantasy child but to a real child to be explored. You are entranced with an intimate stranger. You may experience an odd and intense combination of foreignness and familiarity about this new relationship. As you get to know your baby over the next few weeks, your initial overwhelming tenderness will slowly mature into true love.

Getting Ready

What do you notice about your baby as you lie next to her in bed for hours, look down at her as she breast-feeds, watch her in her sleep? Your eyes are like a telescope on this marvelously miniature human being. You will see things no one else will see and notice odd things that no one else will notice. You are like a scientist and a poet, in awe of the specimen before you. Write what you see.

- The dark gray lint that collects in the lines of his palm.
- How his bent arms and legs, when he is asleep on his stomach, take the shape of an hourglass.
- How he is curious, to the limits of his understanding; how he attempts to approach what arouses his curiosity, to the limits of his motion; how he derives satisfaction from another face opposing itself to his face, to the limits of his attention; how he asserts his needs, to the limits of his force.

—LYDIA DAVIS, "What You Learn"

Journeying

1) Who is this person you are looking at so closely? As you contemplate your small child in silence, you may well wonder from whence he came. Did you choose this spirit or did this spirit choose you? Did the spirit of your child once reside in a close relative or friend now dead? Babies are sometimes con-

ceived at the same time, even on the same day, as the death of a close person in your extended family, which could indicate either a literal or a symbolic transference of spirit. What people does he look like? What ancestors or dream characters do you see in him? What is foreign and what is familiar? Who is this stranger?

2) Your baby isn't the only one with a coming-out story. You, too, will go through a process of coming out publicly into the world as a mother. In this first month, it is a good time to begin this process within the privacy of your nuclear and/or extended family and friends by way of celebration and ceremony. I will give you two suggestions for ceremonies to validate and support your journey into motherhood. The first one I simply call the family ceremony: a ceremony in which you are the queen bee gathering wisdom from your people. I gathered my family together when my son was only two weeks old for a "parenting" ceremony. My son was with us in his plastic baby carrier during the ceremony. As a single mother, I knew that I would not be the only one to parent my child. Different people in my family and some of my friends would also help raise him in different ways. I thought it would be important for them to do some of the thinking that you have been doing in your journal so that they, too, would be more conscious in their parenting. So that they could choose not to repeat any negative parenting they had experienced and would be sure to give my son what they, as children, had found most rewarding. My mother and father were there. My aunt and uncle were there. My brother and sister were there. We each went around and said what the best things were that we learned from or experienced with our parents, what we would never want to repeat with Orlando and how we would choose to be with him.

In addition, we went around the room and each person gave everyone else an appreciation, an important part of any ceremony. By exposing our gratefulness to each other we were able to bond more closely as a family. We were taking the first steps toward building a parenting alliance. I am certain that Orlando heard it all. He remained very peaceful for almost two hours, knowing, on some level, that these people, his new family, intended to take good care of him, to give him their best shot.

When you have completed the ceremony, write down the key things your family does and doesn't want to repeat. You will be able to use these words as reminders later on as I did. My father's bad memories of how his mother embarrassed him in front of others combined with his own naturally shy temperament at an early age has repeatedly kept me from doing the same to my own son: "Say hello to the nice man," etc. I always talk to my son in private about such things and let him just be shy with strangers. I had to let go of feeling embarrassed myself about his "lack of manners" and trusted that he would come out more with new people as his trust of them grew, which is exactly what happened.

A second possible ceremony is a naming ceremony. This could be combined with the family ceremony or could be a separate gathering more with your friends and community, which is what I did. This is a public blessing of the child and a welcome of the new member into the "tribe." This can take many forms: for instance, a Christian baptism is a rite of passage and prepares the child for the grace of God, bringing him into the body of Christ. Different rites and customs are carried out in different cultures. Or you can simply invent your own out of your own spirituality. Let this be a mutual bearing witness between the child and his community. The name of your child becomes the symbol for his entrance into the community. It is a good idea to take this opportunity to bless the parents as well, in acknowledgment of their inner journeys into motherhood and fatherhood, and in honor of their commitment to rearing, with the support of their community, the future of humankind. Think big. Ceremonies put you in touch with all cultures through all time and with the spirit beyond. Write what you learn, what you want to remember from this celebration.

3) Your madonnalike relationship with your baby grows intuitively, innocently without your planning it or even noticing that it is happening. Perhaps it is only your partner or your mother or a friend who suddenly sees the madonna in you, catching a glance of the two of you rocking quietly by the window as if in trance. Stop a minute now and notice for yourself who you have intuitively become in your most private moments with your child. These are the magical, almost transcendent moments when bonding is occurring.

Describe a scene of how the two of you are together, a manifestation of this special bonding.

> I court you to sleep like a lover. I rock and sing and coo and hold you in the special balancing mudra: parallel hands on your rump and upper back. I am quiet and loving for long stretches and then whisper sweet nothings in your ear. I speak to you of romance in Spanish and Italian, addressing each part of your small body. I invite you to dream. I nurse you and let you rest with your mouth on my nipple as you doze so you won't be startled by my bringing you up to be burped on my shoulder, so you can suck softly in your half sleep and let go only when you are ready to, dropping into your deeper sleep. I embrace you there for minutes, or hours, I do not know which for the day feels timeless. Then I lay you down gently in your crib like a china plate onto a glass table. Meticulously, like threading a needle. Strategically, like an experienced mother. I try this numerous times, moving slowly and gracefully as if preparing to defend myself with the ancient martial art of tai chi chuan. But today you cannot rest.
>
> —*Letters to Matagalpa*

4) In celebration of being loved and bonding with others besides your baby, write about your new family, a special way someone is taking care of you and how that feels.

> *A week after our child was born,*
> *you cornered me in the spare room*
> *and we sank down on the bed.*
> *You kissed me and kissed me, my milk undid its*
> *burning slip-knot through my nipples,*

soaking my shirt. All week I had smelled of milk,

fresh milk, sour. I began to throb:

my sex had been torn easily as cloth by the

crown of her head, I'd been cut with a knife and

sewn, the stitches pulling at my skin—

and the first time you're broken, you don't know

you'll be healed again, better than before.

I lay in fear and blood and milk

while you kissed and kissed me, your lips hot and swollen

as a teen-age boy's, your sex dry and big,

all of you so tender, you hung over me,

over the nest of the stitches, over the

splitting and tearing, with the patience of someone who

finds a wounded animal in the woods

and stays with it, not leaving its side

until it is whole, until it can run again.

—SHARON OLDS, "New Mother"

3. Blues

Your sweetness is a burden to me now. . . .

—*Letters to Matagalpa*

Many women with newborns experience what has been termed "the blues," or postpartum depression, a kind of sadness running parallel to the tenderness you wrote about in the last section. Psychologists and others suggest a variety of reasons for this phase in the fourth trimester. Taking a holistic view of your situation means to acknowledge the various contributing factors: physiological, psycho-emotional, and spiritual.

After birth, your hormones don't suddenly settle back into their pre-pregnancy state in the blink of an eye. Your hormone-induced emotional roller coaster isn't quite over. Your emotional life is intense. In addition to the precious love you feel for your baby, you may also be grieving for what you have given up. Spiritual questions may come up: you may experience a bitter-sweet melancholy about the passing of time and your own mortality. The newness of life holds within it its own demise. Looking at your mother, your grandmother, your partner, you may connect more with the sadness of their inevitable passing rather than a celebration of their living.

Some of these feelings may arise from your own feelings of being lost in the strange timelessness of the days seeming to pass you by. As well, you may feel lost as you grapple with your own identity and sense of self. You will be reminded somewhere deep inside you about your own birth and first weeks in this world, and will respond accordingly, depending on the ratio of joy to pain to confusion. Your mood may well be affected by the circumstances of your conception and of your pregnancy, by the very story you have been writing from the beginning of this book. Political questions may come up as you begin to realize the seriousness of your responsibility to this child you have given birth to: what have I done bringing this innocent being into this violent and troubled world?

You may feel let down after all these months of buildup, like those strange moments when all the people are gone from the party and you stand there alone in the absence yet still feel the presence of what had once been. Just like war veterans or anyone who has had a traumatic experience, a new mother may experience a kind of post-traumatic syndrome physically and psychologically.

You are faced with a whole panorama of possible disillusion and disappointment. You may feel the birth experience turned out to be dramatically different than you had hoped, in ways that feel hurtful to yourself or your child. Even though you prepared yourself for any eventuality, you may feel you failed yourself or your child if you took drugs and had wanted a natural birth, or if you were surprised by the need for a cesarean when you'd envisioned a vaginal delivery, or any of many possible deviations from what you had wished. Going over the labor and birth in your mind and in writing, you may wonder: if only I had done this or that, feeling regret or remorse for what may not have been in your control. If you feel this way, it means you have not come to accept what was real and to find the beauty in it.

You may feel disappointed that this is not the child you had imagined. Maybe it doesn't appear to be as "cute" as you had hoped, or you see no resemblance between your child and either parent. Perhaps you expected your baby to give you instant gratification for your labors, a smile or some visible response to your love, and feel disappointed even if you realize that such a "dialogue" is not yet possible. You may be troubled by inexplicable missing pieces to the puzzle of the birth story. Perhaps you are disappointed in the way your partner was with you during the birth or feel abandoned too soon after the birth if he has had to return to work. Perhaps you expected your madonnalike nurturing role to be easy but find breast-feeding to be acutely uncomfortable and discover sleep deprivation is taking its toll. You are in a vulnerable position at this time and with the focus of everyone's attention, that same attention you had basked in just one month ago, being transferred now to the baby, you may well feel invisible and painfully alone.

This is a lot for any one person to handle. Even though you have prepared for it with your writing, you need time to feel what you feel. Your written journey will provide you with understanding and an intelligent and comforting perspective on your blues today. The only solution to these feelings is to express them. These blues too shall pass.

If, however, you don't snap out of it after three to four weeks, seek professional help.

Getting Ready

The blues are like a harmonica chord. The different feelings blend into one mournful tone that is so striking it is difficult to remember that they are actually separate notes played simultaneously. More important than anything else is to write down everything you are feeling without thinking or censoring, and regardless of how irrational it may seem. This is an exercise in exorcism. You must be honest here in the one place you know you can be.

Journeying

You listened to the chord in the last exercise and wrote everything you heard, harmonious and discordant. If it was, in fact, the cacophony one might expect it to be, now is the time to focus on the individual notes carrying the most emotional charge. For myself, one shrill note was political. Having conceived my son in a country of mothers who had lost their sons and daughters to land mines, gunshot, and alcoholism, which, I learned, is the fatal psychological consequence of war, I felt suddenly overwhelmed with the inevitable suffering my innocent baby would experience directly and indirectly in his life. *I give you life and with it a sentence of untold pain. What godforsaken thing have I done?* When we write our feelings down, they no longer own us. The mournful tone becomes a memory woven into the fabric of your life. Suddenly there is psychic space again for your emerging melodies of love and integrated motherhood. Use your "Getting Ready" exercise as a resource. Pull out a specific concern you have and write more fully about it. Pull out another that seems to be pulsing with an electric charge and write about that, too. Put the contents of your depression out on the table for those you trust to see.

Letter to Your Child

Write a letter to your newborn.

Orlando, darling. *You are here.* You have come to meet me eye to eye. You, the littlest person, lie, a miniature human being with your big head on my chest, your skin against my skin. You are not pink, not plastic, not a doll, not a frog, not incomplete or unreal. You are here.

I can feel the weight of you on my body. Your perfect little body is on my own. This is really happening. I heard you cry your first breath. I feel you sucking my nipple as if it belongs to you. I lay back against my pillow, naked under your tiny nakedness, already forgetting the pain of labor, enraptured by your astounding presence. I am amazed how clear it is, a rain-washed sky: there is no turning back. You have entered this world completely. You cannot be wished away as if you were a thought, or hidden like a broken toy. But here. Here for life. The last vestiges of old pain still licking their wounds on the edges of my heart suddenly vanish as if loosened like barnacles from sea rocks. You have come like a current with waves so forceful they snap the suction that had so stubbornly held the pain in place as if it belonged there. You have come like a current, Orlando, and carry it away, out into the deep blue sea, suddenly so light it almost floats, then lighter still so that it seems to fly. I welcome you with an open heart.

—*Letters to Matagalpa*

Eleven

Down Under

Your Eleventh Month

There is no greater happiness than giving birth and then rising in love with a human being of your own making—helpless, vulnerable, and sweet. On the other hand, at least sixteen waking hours per day (not to mention a few hours a night) can easily be filled up with diapering, feeding, cleaning up, a little cooing and chitchat, responding to a phenomenally large vocabulary of crying, assisting your baby into sleep, changing clothes, washing clothes, drying clothes, and breast-feeding. The same dependency that feels endearing can also become a noose around your neck.

Your darling baby is precious without a doubt. On the other hand, no other relationship exists in which the unspoken rules governing "personal space" are so flagrantly disregarded. You may feel your breasts are not your breasts anymore but belong instead to your baby. Meanwhile, while you have had body contact all day, your partner, who may be in particular need of your love and may well feel excluded from your special relationship with the baby, wants your touch. You may feel used, buried in the needs of everyone else while your own needs are probably not getting met.

Internally, you are begging to be esteemed, noticed, cared for. The situation may feel as if it's zooming out of control. That nothing will ever be the same again bangs on your heart like sleet on the roof. You are completely exhausted, healing, and with little sleep. Surviving hour by hour, your days are flooded with milk, excrement, blood, urine, and spit. This is the pure taste of motherhood. Just as your emperor wears new clothes, you are grieving for the life you had. "I never imagined it would be like this" is a common chant among mothers with their first newborn.

You are in the thick of integrating your new role of motherhood with an ongoing sense of self, but for the moment, that self feels completely swallowed up. This is the flip side of your madonna self. Paradox after paradox begins to strip your heart of its initial innocence.

The first weeks after birth is the period our society has aptly called "confinement" with all its negative connotations. Whereas examples of societies that create a position of honor and comfort for new mothers do exist, particularly in agricultural cultures and traditions, our industrialized society tends to isolate us. We as people have lost our intuitive honoring of the mother just as we have lost much of our land to concrete, quarries, and stumps.

A time of honoring and comfort is something we have to create for ourselves, just as we created ceremony and built alliances among family and friends before the birth. Use your words. Don't ignore your yearning for one thing and one thing only: time alone. Experience this desire as a directive. Don't be democratic about it. Dictate. This will be your time to reflect, to connect with yourself, to write. Even if you feel as though you're drowning, even if it is for a few minutes only, do the impossible. A few words will make a big difference.

1. Pure Taste of Motherhood

Days into weeks.
Still night sweats
and bleeding still,
its bleachy smell.
Your bleat softly
shears the thick
fleece of dark.
I wake wet,

cold, hot:

milk and sweat,

nightgown, hair,

humid breasts.

Here you are.

——RACHEL HADAS,
"Up and Down"

On the other side of tenderness are urine-soaked diapers. On the other side of the sweet maternal feelings you wrote about in the last chapter are resentment, frustration, awkwardness, and the inconvenience of twenty-four-hour baby care. In this section, you can complain about the tedium and daily trials of very early parenting and indulge in feeling trapped in it. You are, as poet Adrienne Rich has put it, "diving into the wreck." Your pen is your oxygen tank. You will come up.

Getting Ready

Start out with a free write. Fill it with the sensory details of the contained and intimate domestic world you feel funneled into. Don't stop with one smell. Include all the smells and all their nuances. Write down the tastes, the seemingly infinite variety of sounds and textures. Milk, excrement, tears, tongues, sweat.

> The baby cries. You wake and rise to feed her. The sky has just begun to lighten behind the blind, and in the grainy bedroom light, you can see her one-eyed sideways blue stare above your breast, hunger even more intense than love.
>
> —JOYCE THOMPSON, "Dreams of a New Mother"

Journeying

1) Divulge the flip side of your madonna. Write how you feel about your "confinement."

Today I have done nothing. But be with you. I have eaten nothing. I have not left you. I sit in my loose blue shirt drenched halfway down with milk, fresh milk that has wet through the dried milk spots from last night's milkings. And I cry. I never stop loving you for a minute. I know we both want you with all our hearts to sleep. I cry, Orlando, because I cannot move and I do not know if I will ever be able to move. I feel trapped in the tree house I have made for you. I feel there is no exit to these long moments, that this day will go into night and into the next day and into the weeks and years ahead ad infinitum. My frustration grows from a tree into a forest and then spreads like timber over all the mountains I can see, not even leaving the pure white snowy peaks to rest a hope on. Then, slowly, all the trees fall, one after the other, crashing down into the center of pure sorrow.

You and I alone in this small room. Alone in the world. I have made you and now you make me.

—*Letters to Matagalpa*

2) Boundaries are shifting. Normal mundane things like being able to eat a meal with two hands on the table feels like sheer luxury. Nine out of ten times the free hand is needed to hold the suckling baby (even though it is already stuffed to the gills with your milk) so that you can at least eat that one dab of mashed potatoes with melted butter on it before giving up on dinner for the night again. Find the humor in your misery. What, when you step back from it for a moment, would actually be hilarious to recount if only it were happening to someone else?

2. Locating Ourselves: A Changing Identity

I turned to that self inside me, that girlwoman who had once been all I needed to know of myself, whom I had fought to understand, to love, to free—I turned to her now and I banished her. Into a protective shell tied in a knot, she retreated, four, five, six times a day, whenever Benjamin wanted to nurse. Soon, even when I sought her, she would not come, but began to stay out of reach longer and longer, sometimes not reappearing for whole days. For if she was present when the baby needed me, she was of necessity pushed aside, sent to go hungry. She who had been my life, whom I knew I had to nourish daily in order to be fed in return, hid for weeks, hoarding her gentleness and her strength, placing no gifts in my outstretched hands.

—JANE LAZARRE, "The Mother Knot"

The most challenging miles you will walk on any journey into a new identity are *after* the actual change of circumstance takes place and *just before* you actually integrate and accept the new identity. Take marriage, for example. A woman's identity shift into bride, wife, or mate doesn't occur with a snap the very moment the rings are exchanged. Nor does it happen during the honeymoon, well stocked as it is with romantic illusions. There is a point, however, during every honeymoon when we look each other full in the face as if for the first time. Reality descends. Even light seems to alter its intensity. We suddenly see what we have gone and done. *This is when the work begins.*

With a baby, the honeymoon can last a few days or a few weeks, but sooner or later, coming to terms with one's new identity becomes the dominant psychological theme. Although you have been coming to terms with what it means to become a mother for nine months, actually *being* a mother brings everything into crystal clear focus. This is your reality. Nothing is blurred anymore.

First, you will experience the inevitable struggle between the old and new identities and then, just before the moment of acceptance, right at the end of the process of integration, the old self will cry out like a child caught in a rip tide, overwhelmed with the feeling that she is being pulled out to sea. The ego doesn't seem to understand that integration results in depth and expansion. It simply feels that it will die and will flail at the ocean's huge surface in a panic to avoid this. These are the internal battles your writing will assist you with during your "confinement." Integration lies peacefully within your reach.

Journeying

1) *Paradox*, from the Greek, means "beyond opinion," and the paradox is this: How can I be myself and be this mother both at the same time? How can they coexist? Or are they mutually exclusive? Can I be sexual and be a mother? Can I be professionally ambitious and be a mother? Can I be two people? Does one get lost when the other is claimed? How can I wed them or blend them in a way that expands my sense of self while staying utterly connected to the heart of who I am and always have been? You have written about these concerns during your pregnancy. Now you have a new perspective. You are unequivocally a mom. Stop a moment to notice the war that may be raging in your psyche. In what ways are your merging identities manifesting struggle, striving for individual recognition, or happily congruent? Write for twenty minutes. Remember that this paradox of roles and selves will never completely go away. These are questions your journal will continue to bear witness to as the months blend into years. Remember, too, that your new paradoxical identity is beyond opinion. In that sense, you are like God: you simply *are*.

> I felt I should never have had a baby. If anyone had told me what it would be like, I might have saved my life in time. Who was this immensely powerful person, screaming unintelligibly, sucking my breast until I was in a state of fatigue the likes of which I had never known?

Who was he and by what authority had he claimed the right to my life? I would never be a good mother. . . . As he drew milk out of me, my inner self seemed to shrink into a very small knot, gathering intensity under a protective shell, moving away, further and further away, from the changes being wrought by this child who was at once separate and a part of me. Frightened that he would claim my life completely, I desperately tried to cling to my boundaries. Yet I held him very close, stroked his skin, imagined that we were still one person.

—JANE LAZARRE, "The Mother Knot"

2) Still there is a life and a self that this life revolved around that you must say good-bye to. Just as you are in love, you are in mourning. If you don't say good-bye to what is truly gone, you may cling to it and it will be a burden to you. Not unlike a human death, the body may be gone, but the spirit is there—together with memories and ineffable influences. You may well experience the same stages of mourning you would if a parent died. Denial. Anger. Sadness. Acceptance. It will be important for you to express these feelings as they come up, to validate them with your words. They may seem irreverent or feel selfish and mean. But mourning is a natural part of all significant processes of change. Just as a woman cannot carry an old boyfriend or ex-husband into a new fabulous relationship. She must say good-bye to something that no longer exists in the form in which it once existed. It is the form we say good-bye to.

Sit silently with yourself for a few minutes. What do you feel you have actually lost? Allow yourself to mourn.

Looking at the Map

All is not lost. When you get your bearings down under, you can easily navigate up, straight to the surface where sunlight is dancing into sparkles. Rip off your oxygen tank and take a deep breath of fresh ocean air. Notice the huge world around you. In the next chapter, you will pay attention not to what you've lost in the shuffle, but to what you've gained.

Letter to Your Child

Write a letter to your child from down under.

Dear Orlando Kirk,

It is now, when the city is asleep, that finally I can be with myself. It is in these three hours of quiet time, when you, too, Orlando, are asleep, that I can reflect. I can look back at my day and realize that I never really needed to leave your tree house today. That I could have easily survived without eating for one day and that I would still have had enough milk for you. That I didn't need a shower, or have to make a phone call or pay a bill or have to accomplish anything. I realize because my love grows for you the more I take the time to watch and understand you, to listen to your tiny talking and loud crying lungs, that this day is not my whole life, that another day will follow it when I will not be alone with you, and that the only thing I really need to do now is take care of you.

You are the door. The exit and the entrance. Today I cried because I was terrified that I was losing myself. But I cannot lose in one day what I have been building for thirty-six years. And you, little one, less than five weeks old, need me to be with you. I hear you crying now on the mark for something I carry in my breast but cannot invent with words.

—*Letters to Matagalpa*

Twelve

Full Circle

Your First Year

You have come full circle from conception. One year has passed since your journey into motherhood literally began. Two months have passed since you gave birth to your child. If you have not already done so, you will soon end your period of "confinement." On the anniversary of your child's conception, you come out of the womb of your home and enter the public world *a mother*.

These are the weeks when things start to settle. Weary but wiser with practice, the physical act of mothering is not so foreign to you. It may take you ten times longer to get out of the house, but the details are second nature to you now. The initial shock is over along with the novelty. As you move from the private and into the public sphere, you enter various stages of separation from your baby. Though you are physically separated at birth, your identities often remain merged for weeks in a highly symbiotic relationship. Now something changes. Both you and your baby are likely to become interested in something other than each other. Your baby may stare in fascination at her own fists or kick her legs with devoted energy, bicycling into another stratosphere, discovering her own power to influence the universe. You, too, are in for the treat of discovery as you reposition yourself in your new life, reconnecting yourself to the web of your earlier existence: friends, family, work, health and finances, your spiritual and social communities.

Stepping into the world as a mother, however, doesn't automatically mean you have arrived at the end of your journey into motherhood. There is a big difference between existing in the world of motherhood by default (I must be a mother because I have a son) and actually claiming it. That difference is integration. Your journey ends only when you embrace your motherhood identity utterly and completely.

Integrating means becoming whole again. To become whole requires untold courage—the courage to let go of what was, and to accept something else—not resignation, not tolerance, but a profound and decisive acceptance of something new. Letting go of an attachment, whether that attachment feels positive (I want to be happy) or negative (I don't want to feel sad anymore), allows something different to take its place. This is both the hardest and the easiest thing to do. We can decide today to let go of a particular identity or expectation and claim instead the unfolding of the deeper vision we carry in our hearts.

In the section called "Courtship: Down on Our Knees," we start the end of our journey by acknowledging love, both our maturing mother love for our babies and our maturing love for ourselves as mothers. In the section called "Courage and Acceptance," we move to culminate our journey by locating ourselves in this new present time and by making the choice to embrace our motherhood completely. The paradox is this: By actively embracing motherhood, we do not lose or diminish our commitment to our sense of self but strengthen it.

As you step out into the world again, the world will ask you, Are you willing to accept this commitment to your motherhood and yourself *simultaneously* for richer or for poorer, in sickness and in health, until death do you part? And you will say: I do.

1. Courtship: Down on Our Knees

As your childbearing year comes to an end, you can celebrate your anniversary with your child. Your relationship with your embryo, your fetus, and now your baby has been honest, intimate, and deep from the beginning. You emerge now from your first two months of being a mother like a seal out of the sea. Shiny and distinct, you climb out onto the rocks. You leave behind you the simplicity of the pure and innocent love of a madonna. You leave behind you the melancholy of the blues and the initial overwhelming pungency of actual motherhood. As you lie now on your rock in the sun, you embrace a new sense of space and time. Next to you is another seal. Separate and distinct. Your baby. Your feelings for him feel different now as you experience him as absolutely other. Soon you will watch him crawl away from you across the wide green expanse of a park without once looking back, ride a bicycle alone down the street, go to his first day of school. When you recognize your baby as an individual person, separate from yourself, you inevitably experience a different quality of love. Your love for your child has been growing and maturing for months. You have imagined it, dreamed, it, been enamored of a spirit no one could see. Your love has brandished the brilliant flags of infatuation and has wandered aimlessly in and out of enchantment.

Now it is real.

How can you not get down on your knees?

Journeying

1) In the first weeks, your baby was still a stranger, a human specimen to observe like a scientist in awe and wonder. Now she is no longer foreign to you. The caliber of your love seems to multiply with each hour, increasing exponentially. Your relationship with your infant is like every relationship in that your love, with time, becomes more authentic. And yet it is unlike any relationship you have ever had before. Notice everything about your new child. Each smell, each sound, each movement, and the texture of his skin. Notice everything about how you feel about him. It seems inexpressible. Yet now you have had months of practice translating the unspeakable into words. Write love letters and poems to your little one—down on your knees.

> The heart of speech beats in your small chest, trying to get out. Like the ocean searching to escape through crevices of shore rocks fallen tightly together extending the land out to the sea. Your speech is breath. Air from your chest almost empty of sound, pushing hard as if to pick up tones like sediment stuck to the sides of your throat,

jollying your voice box into activity. You are a gold digger panning for gold, scavenging the river bottom for the heaviest little sound, not the sand and silt that is silent but the nuggets, audible shapes of precious speech. I hear the iron pan scratching against the sand and mossy rocks but nothing shiny comes out; just a few squeaks, fool's gold. Your own little wind hurdles again from your gut through tubes, funnels into your throat, and blows out in small gusts of muted language. Your own breath is the eye of your storming mouth, pushing, pushing it out until suddenly there it is: a word that I cannot understand. The sound of water over a spoon. Not a coo, not like the pigeons do, not like the doves. Never the same sound twice. You explore without reservation the delicate phonetics that carve the space in front of you. An orchestra now of sound, pianissimo, fortissimo, always allegro. And I, in love, have watched you move from speechlessness to speech.

—*Letters to Matagalpa*

2) Now that your baby lies there in her crib, in your arms, on the couch, so clearly separate from yourself, not just a strange guest in the house, but your daughter or your son, you realize she has her own thoughts, her own feelings, her own personality. The compassion training you did during your pregnancy with your mother and your partner has taught you how to get inside another person as part of a process of individuation in order to understand them better and thus to love them better. Now you can use your training to get into the impossibly tiny shoes of your baby. Imagine you are her. Write from your baby's point of view.

I lie in my crib midday this is

unusual I don't sleep really

Mamma's sweeping or else boiling water for tea

Other sounds are creak of chair & floor, water

    dripping on heater from laundry, cat licking itself. . . .

She takes me through a door, a wind howls

    Furry shapes & large vehicles move close

I'm squinting, light cuts through my skin

    World is vast I'm in it with closed eyes. . . .

Water is soft I came from water

    Not that long ago I was inside her

like flames, the cat pouncing, shadows or light

streaming in

    I heard her voice then I remember now. . . .

—ANNE WALDMAN, "Baby's Pantoum"

3) Now that you are a mother, you need more support than you could have ever imagined. Remember the job description for mothering that you wrote in Chapter Five "Redefining Motherhood"? With little or no training, you are doing that job now, full-time, overtime, all the time. You join forces with millions of mothers, the unsung heroines populating our common history. You deserve acknowledgment for your work. If no one has thought to give it to you, ask for it. Find at least one person, your partner or a friend, that you can brag to every day about one parenting victory, someone who can also listen attentively to ten minutes of disappointments and complaints without interrupting. Although you could certainly benefit from having someone help you figure things out right now, that is not your number-one priority. What you need is validation, affirmation, reassurance, and acknowledgment.

You need a place to vent your daily frustrations so that you can think more clearly. You need praise. Ask for what you need from the people closest to you. Make a habit of writing love letters to yourself. Start right now. Acknowledge yourself for your fine mothering, for each small success, for giving birth to a healthy human being with unlimited potential! Write for as long as you need to.

2. Locating Ourselves: Courage and Acceptance

> Everything seems different this morning. Something is about to happen, something startling or maybe just exciting. A change in the air, in my mind, something I woke up with and have carried ever since.
>
> —CAROLE ITTER, "Cry Baby"

Life after your first year will be a time of integration of worlds and selves. You are integrating the inner journey of the last twelve months with the realities of your external world. You are integrating motherhood with everything you have ever understood you are in that world: your purpose, your place, your passion, your soul.

Practicing motherhood requires spiritual, emotional, and physical stamina; a high tolerance for uncertainty, unpredictability, and imprecision; and a well-developed sense of humor. You will be your child's teacher just as your mother and father have been yours. You will model the values you believe in and prepare him for a life in a beautiful, troubled, and increasingly complex world. You will manifest your new definition of motherhood, a combination of the one you imagined in Chapter Five plus the one that evolves daily inside you.

Our children inherit the future we create. We have a responsibility to our children and to our planet to take the future seriously, not to settle for anything less than absolutely everything, and to act in the world as agents of change.

Take a moment to feel the immensity of the task before you.

As you begin your parenting journey, you may take great courage from the thinking, feeling, and writing you have already done. You have given testimony to who you were when this journey began and located your motherhood path on your mythical life map. You have acknowledged, loved, and honored your intelligent body. You have located yourself and your child's new life in relation to the world, your ancestry, and your own personal past. You have strengthened your relationship with your mother, your father, and your partner. You have evolved an understanding of what kind of mother you intend to be and have gained the confidence to exercise that powerful vision. You have celebrated yourself as the queen that you are, experienced yourself connected rather than isolated, and built a support system, no matter how large or small, that you can count on. Most important, you have been honest. You have cared enough about life to reflect on it and feel it deeply with your words. You have developed the journaling habit for years to come.

All of this you take with you for the rest of your parenting life.

As your train pulls into this station, the station that marks off the beginning of the rest of your life, the journal work you have done will reward you with a kind of deep inner peace. Not that everything has been resolved, but that you are wholly in your life, a life that you have come to understand and clearly see even as it continues changing. You feel ready to accept it. Acceptance brings closure. Closure brings peace. Motherhood has become something you believe is unalterably true and you receive it willingly like a gift.

Journeying

1) It's coming-out time. Not the baby coming out of you but you coming out of the house, out of the cave, out of the timeless world you've been inhabiting. You have been looking inward for many weeks. It is healthy to begin to look out the window, to notice how you fit into the big world out there. Focus on this new crossroad in your life just as you did in your first month from a premotherhood perspective. Write about your key relationships, your

work, your health, your plans, your spirituality. Get a bearing on your current reality from an outer as well as an inner focus.

2) Whereas before, for years and years, you walked down the street with only a purse stuffed with a comb, some change, and a couple of credit cards, now you have a bag of provisions to last a few days and your child in your arms. Write about how you feel "coming out" as a mother.

3) Your baby is separate from you. Remember the Kahlil Gibran poem in *The Prophet?* "Our children are ours yet we do not own them. You may house their bodies but not their souls." Write down a moment in which you really felt, perhaps for the first time, that you could see your child as a whole person and recognized that you are two separate beings on different paths. Write from your heart how this revelation makes you feel.

> *My daughter's pajamas lie on the floor*
>
> *inside out, thin and wrinkled as*
>
> *peeled skins of peaches when you ease the*
>
> *whole skin off at once.*
>
> *You can see where her waist emerged, and her legs,*
>
> *her arms, and head, the fine material*
>
> *gathered in rumples like the skin the caterpillar*
>
> *ramped out of and left to shrivel.*
>
> *You can see, there at the center of the bottoms,*
>
> *the raised cotton seam like the line*
>
> *down the center of fruit, where the skin first splits*
>
> *and curls back. You can almost see the hard*
>
> *halves of her young buttocks, the precise*

Leslie Kirk Campbell

stem-mark of her sex. Her shed

skin shines at my feet, and in the air there is a

sharp fragrance like peach brandy—

the birth-room pungence of released life.

—SHARON OLDS, "Pajamas"

4) There will be a moment when it all comes together, when the worlds and the selves are integrated and you feel whole again. No one can say that this moment will come like clockwork on the anniversary of your child's conception. Acceptance cannot be scheduled in. We can move toward it, yet we cannot embrace it until we are ready

It took five years for me to embrace my motherhood completely. Until the day I was able to receive motherhood as a gift, I felt that I would die if I totally took on the identity of mother. Attached to an idea of my premotherhood self as being freewheeling, adventuresome, bohemian, artistic, and totally adult, I was stubborn for years and refused to do it. My psychic wrestling was not obvious to the outside world. I looked like a good mother. But I learned my lesson. I learned that you can't go through the motions of motherhood without claiming it in your heart and still raise a healthy child. My son had become angry for good reason and did not feel the extra specialness that was his birthright. You can't hide anything from a child. Babies and toddlers know more than we think. They don't filter emotional information through thought and language the way we do. They simply know it in their hearts.

When integration finally came to me, it came to me in a flash, one of those landmark revelatory moments that changes your life forever. It came to me because my own journey into motherhood had come to feel like a dead end: my son and I were angry and unhappy in it. Change comes to us when we are ready for it. The emergency sirens may be blasting but we only look at the disaster when we have the courage to pay attention to it or when we feel we have no other choice. I confess my change came as a consequence of the latter. When push came to shove, I chose life over death, love over pain, happiness over anger. It was only when I was able to claim my motherhood 100 percent that I was able to experience the love that had always been there between myself and my son. I call it my lemon-tree epiphany because it happened with my best friend in her backyard with the lemons lit up all around us by southern California sunlight. The form of my life had changed dramatically since I had given birth. No question. But the miracle is this: When I claimed my motherhood that afternoon, my self expanded. "I" did not die, as I had desperately feared. I simply unfolded. I became more beautifully and completely myself and the world responded with gifts of love, success, and a satisfaction deeper than any I had ever known.

Now I am myself and I am mother. I wrestle with parenting choices daily but the inner war is over. Chances are your journey into wholeness will be swifter than mine. I congratulate you in advance on your arrival into motherhood, that unutterably beautiful, constantly evolving, profoundly real world that you clearly belong to.

❧

When you are ready, write a meditation out of acceptance. Allow your words to give you closure. A year ago you wrote a dedication for your journal, proclaiming your purpose. Read your dedication and let yourself feel the power of your own courage and the sacredness of the work you have done. You have been invited to enter the world of motherhood with your heart and mind completely intact. Write a letter to the world: your letter of acceptance.

Letter to Your Child

Write an anniversary letter to your child. Then close your journal. Feel the power of the silence. Your journey is done and it is never done. You have given birth to a new mother and here you are, the wiser for your words, the book that you have written resting before you. As you go into your second year, pen in hand, you will not be alone. We will be with you. Myself, all the women who have contributed to this book, all the women who are using it as you do, and the millions more who have taken pen to paper while bearing and raising their children everywhere in the world and throughout history. We will be with you.

Dear Orlando,

Today I have in mind—you the man. I imagine you with your thick dark hair sitting on a brick wall, your long legs dangling, reading these letters. Today I want to celebrate us. We have come full circle. We are ready, like the Greek snake Ouroboros, to hold our tails in our mouths. We have met our end and our end is our beginning. There is nowhere to go and everywhere to go. We hold the dark and the light in the palms of our hands.

—*Letters to Matagalpa*

Weeks 1–12

$\mathcal{A}$ppendix

Recommended Reading

The following are a few very readable and enjoyable books that I have found which focus on the inner journey of pregnancy and early motherhood. Some of these are based on psychological research, some on sociological, historical, or anthropological studies, some on private workshop experience, and some are simply writings by women whose journeys into motherhood moved them to write poems, stories, and to reflect with their words on their condition. Each one of these books has been an inspiration to me in my own journey and has contributed greatly to the writing of this book.

1. Block, Joyce, Ph.D. *Motherhood as Metamorphosis: Change and Continuity in the Life of a New Mother.* New York: Penguin Books Inc., Plume, 1990.

2. Chester, Laura; editor. *Cradle and All: Women Writers on Pregnancy and Birth.* Boston: Faber and Faber, 1989.

3. Colman, Libby Lee, Ph.D. and Arthur D. Colman, M.D. *Pregnancy: The Psychological Experience.* New York: Farrar, Straus and Giroux, Noonday Press, 1991.

4. Dally, Ann. *Inventing Motherhood: The Consequences of an Ideal.* New York: Schocken Books, 1982.

5. Dunham, Carroll and The Body Shop Team. *Mamatoto: A Celebration of Birth.* New York: Penguin Books Inc., Viking, 1991.

6. Hegland, Jean. *The Life Within.* Clifton, New Jersey: Humana Press, 1991.

7. McMahon, Peggy O'Mara, Editor. *Mother Poet.* Albuquerque, New Mexico: Mothering Publications, Inc., 1983.

8. Otten, Charlotte, Editor. *The Book of Birth Poetry.* New York: Bantam Books, 1995.

9. Panuthos, Claudia. *Transformation Through Birth: A Woman's Guide.* New York: Bergin and Garvey, 1984.

10. Schwartz, Leni. *Bonding Before Birth: A Guide to Becoming a Family.* Boston: Sigo Press, 1991.

11. Stern, Ellen Sue. *Expecting Change: The Emotional Journey Through Pregnancy.* New York: Bantam Books, 1986.

Credits

Marlene Anne Bumganer: "Creation" printed by permission of the author.

Phyllis Capello: "Listen . . ." printed by permission of the author.

Barbara Crooker: "Freight Train" Copyright © 1983. Used by permission of *McCalls.*

Lydia Davis: "What You Learn" printed by permission of the author.

Diane di Prima: "The Loba Sings to Her Cub" from *Loba* (Wingbow Press, 1978). Copyright © 1978 by Diane di Prima. Reprinted by permission of the author.

Gail Rudd Entrekin: "This Time" Copyright © 1993 by Gail Rudd Entrekin. Reprinted by permission of the author.

Doris Ferleger: Excerpt from "Emptying" printed by permission of the author.

Kathleen Fraser: Excerpt from "What I Want" Copyright © 1974 by Kathleen Fraser. Used by permission of Marian Reiner for the author.

Bobi Jones: "Portrait of a Pregnant Woman" from *Bobi Jones Selected Poems,* tr. Joseph P. Clancy, Christopher Davies Publishers Ltd. Reprinted by permission and Copyright © the publisher 1987.

Rachel Hadas: "Up and Down" from *A Son from Sleep* Copyright © 1987 by Rachel Hadas, Wesleyan University Press. Used by permission of University Press of New England.

Jean Hegland: Excerpts from *The Life Within* Copyright © 1991 by Jean Hegland. Reprinted by permission of the Humana Press.

Helen Hoffman: "Night Journey" Copyright © 1984 by Helen Hoffman. Reprinted by permission of the editor of the *Ohio Review* and the author.

Jane Lazarre: Excerpt from *The Mother Knot*, Copyright © 1976 by Jane Lazarre. Printed by permission of the author.

Jessica Murray: Excerpt from "Elsa's Birth" used by permission of the author.

Joan Rohr Myers: "Fertility" Copyright Commonweal Foundation © 1985. Reprinted by permission of Commonweal Foundation.

Sharon Olds: "The Moment the Two Worlds Meet" from *The Gold Cell*, by Sharon Olds. Copyright © 1987 by Sharon Olds. Reprinted by permission of Alfred A. Knopf, Inc.

"New Mother" and "Pajamas" from *The Dead and the Living* by Sharon Olds. Copyright © 1983 by Sharon Olds. Reprinted by permission of Alfred A. Knopf, Inc.

"The Planned Child" from *The Wellspring* by Sharon Olds. Copyright © 1996 by Sharon Olds. Reprinted by permission of Alfred A. Knopf, Inc.

Mary Ellis Peterson: "Conception" from *Motherpoet,* Copyright © 1983 and *And I Shall Be Your Ancestor,* Copyright © 1980. Printed by permission of the author.

Barbara Ras: Excerpt from "Pregnant Poets Swim Lake Tarleton, New Hampshire" Copyright *Massachusetts Review* © 1988. Used by permission of *The Massachusetts Review.*

Susan Suntree: "Birthing Brings Me" from *Eye of the Womb,* Power Press, Copyright © 1981. Used by permission of the author.

Anne Waldman: "Enceinte" and excerpt from "Baby's Pantoum" from *First Baby Poems* (Rocky Ridge Cottage Editions, 1982; Hyacinth Girls Editions, 1983). Copyright © 1982, 1983 by Anne Waldman. Reprinted by permission of the author.

Al Young: "For Arl in Her Sixth Month" from *Birth Poetry,* Second Coming Press, Copyright © 1976 by Al Young. Reprinted with permission of the author.